D1244225

NEEDLE FELTING

from Ducks to Dragons, Bears, Minis & More

Step-by-step instructions for each creature, plus techniques for layering, 3-D effects & more

Liza Adams

STACKPOLE
BOOKS
Guilford, Connecticut

Published in North America by Stackpole Books
An imprint of The Rowman & Littlefield Publishing Group, Inc.
4501 Forbes Blvd., Ste. 200
Lanham, MD 20706
www.rowman.com

Distributed by NATIONAL BOOK NETWORK
800-462-6420

Text copyright © Liza Adams, 2020
Typographical design copyright © David Bateman Ltd., 2020
Photographs copyright © Liza Adams, 2020

All rights reserved. No part of this book may be reproduced in any form or by any electronic or mechanical means, including information storage and retrieval systems, without written permission from the publisher, except by a reviewer who may quote passages in a review.

The contents of this book are for personal use only. Patterns herein may be reproduced in limited quantities for such use. Any large-scale commercial reproduction is prohibited without the written consent of the publisher.

We have made every effort to ensure the accuracy and completeness of these instructions. We cannot, however, be responsible for human error, typographical mistakes, or variations in individual work.

No responsibility for loss caused to any individual or organization acting on or refraining from action as a result of the material in this publication can be accepted by Stackpole Books, David Bateman Ltd., or the author.

British Library Cataloguing in Publication Information available

ISBN 978-0-8117-3882-8 (paper : alk. paper)

Library of Congress Cataloging-in-Publication Data

Library of Congress Control Number: 2020940594

CONTENTS

INTRODUCTION

BEGINNER PROJECTS

INTERMEDIATE PROJECTS

ADVANCED PROJECTS

EXTRA IDEAS FOR FUN

ABOUT THE BOOK

In my second book about how to needle felt, I wanted to extend my readers/craftspeople to try something new. This book includes some amazing projects to really get you thinking about what else you can do with this craft. If you didn't work through the first book, *Needle Felting From Basics to Bears*, it would be a great place to start, but if you want to begin with this one you can. All the information is there to get you started even if you haven't felted before. Because I take you step-by-step, with insider information and techniques, anyone can pick up this craft and create something wonderful and unique!

BEGINNER PROJECTS

The first two projects teach you how to felt. As you work through them, making a Character Ball and a Curled-up Critter, you will learn how to work with fiber and get a general idea of how much loose fiber is needed to create the piece as you go.

You will learn how to start by winding your fiber for the ball, and how to work it into shape for the critter. You will learn how to cover the core of your work and how to layer up and edge eyeballs as you create your Character Ball.

With the Curled-up Critter, you will discover how you can coax the fiber into shape, working slowly, and how to add details like ears and tails.

I hope you enjoy the beginning of your fiber journey. If you love these two projects, take a look at my first book, where you can learn to make a cupcake, an ornament and a brooch, along with other fun ideas!

INTERMEDIATE PROJECTS

The next three projects are going to be a bit trickier! Take your time, and make more than one if you wish before moving on. Each project brings new ideas and techniques for you to try. Tabby Cat helps you to make your first jointed creature; you will be sculpting each part of the cat and then thread jointing it together. You will learn how to give him stripes and how to make his super cute little face.

Dizzy Duck is totally different. His webbed feet and wings will be something new to try. You will also learn my very own technique to add weight to your work. This allows items to sit better and gives a different feel to your work. You can use it on almost anything you create! Then Elle Elephant brings new limb shapes, head shape and ear shapes. There is so much to try! And you also get a taste for making tiny clothes, as we make a simple dress for her to wear.

ADVANCED PROJECTS

The most advanced project in the book is the gorgeous Denny Dragon. With his super-sculpted head and muzzle, his unique body shape, spikes and rolls you will really be stretching yourself as you make a very special little creation that you can enjoy for yourself or give as a special gift.

The Micro Bee Bear is super small, and you will be taking all that you have learned on earlier projects and using it to create arms and legs on a tiny scale (and you will need to joint them too!). Working on this very small scale is more difficult than you might think, but the results can be very pleasing.

EXTRA IDEAS FOR FUN

Our last two projects are totally different. You will learn how to work over pipe cleaners with Lady Linara, as well as how to work on a larger scale, and make sweet friends for young and old alike.

The last project, Pots of Joy, will give you ideas for making your own miniature scenes and gardens in small cups, vases, pots, or whatever you like! These fun projects extend what you have already learned and give you ideas for other ways to work with fiber.

If you already have book one, *Needle Felting From Basics to Bears*, you will love book two. Each project will teach you something different. If this is your first time needle felting, you will love learning these techniques and following the step-by-step instructions and photos. And if you enjoy this book, I hope you will consider adding my first book to your collection, as you will learn even more by having the set! Happy felting!

Liza Adams

Little Handfuls
MINI BEARS

WHAT IS NEEDLE FELTING?

I always find this to be rather a big question. It is just something that I do, and after doing it for so long it has become second nature to me. I don't tend to think about how I do it. This makes the process of writing instructions a good exercise for me! But even then, I can tell you how to needle felt more easily than I can explain what it is.

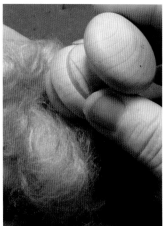

There are a number of basic descriptions, and if asked at a show I will usually say: "Needle felting is taking loose fiber, mixing it all up and then poking it with special needles. These needles have unique shafts with various barbs along them. Poking these in and out of the fiber will cause it to tangle up, and as the fibers tangle they compact down and get firmer. In this way, needle felters are able to sculpt the fiber into the shape they want."

I say sculpt because that is really what we are doing. Once you start working with the needles and fibers, you will see what I mean. I find that when I start a piece it is very soft and has no shape or substance but as I work it there comes a point where it firms up and is able to be sculpted.

Perhaps in this way it is similar to a sculptor working with clay; you have to prepare the clay, whatever kind you are using, so that it is ready to be worked into something amazing. It is the same with the fiber. Once it is holding together, you can manipulate and sculpt with the needle to get it into the shape you need. No matter what size you like to work in, the premise is the same, but remember that the more wool you use, the longer it takes!

Needle felting is a very unusual craft, unlike any other I have done. I love teaching it and hearing from my students how their friends and families react when they go home after their first lesson. Most come back the next week and say, "No one knows what I'm talking about!" Needle felting is just one of those things that makes more sense when you see it rather than hear about it. Though I will never forget the woman who came up to me at a show and, after watching for a few minutes, said: "So if I poke at some wool with a needle it will turn into a bear?" From memory, my reply was to stutter and stammer my way through the above description as I was so surprised at her take on the situation. But what I really wanted to say was: "Only in the same way that if you water bare earth it will turn into a wonderful garden!"

You have to have skill, talent and knowledge to create something wonderful from nothing, and I hope to help you achieve your own wonderful creations in the following pages.

NEEDLES

I try to keep the tools as simple as possible. You need felting needles, naturally, but there are over 30 grades of needle and every country has different grading systems and sizes. This can get complicated, so in this book I work with just two needles — one larger and one smaller.

Also, needles *will* break. You may break *many* needles. Some of my students have broken two or three every lesson for the first few weeks. It just depends on your technique as you learn. Once you refine your methods, breakages are much less common.

You need to experiment for yourself, see what needles are available and how they work with the fiber you can source. Balancing the needles and the fiber is important. Your choice of needle will depend on the grade of fiber. If you can only source coarse fiber, you won't want to use fine needles as they will take a very long time to compact your fiber down into something you can work with. What should only take you four hours will end up taking six or more. Conversely, if you can only source lovely fine merino fiber you won't want to be using very big needles as the fiber will resist the bigger needles and not felt down at all.

I didn't use merino for years, as I found it hard to work with and it took so much longer to get firm. But you have to work with what you can; as long as you can match your needles to your fiber that will be a good start.

In the book I use a 36T, a 38T and a 40T. The 36T is the larger needle and the T stands for triangle. There are also star-shaped and other shaped needles for specific tasks, such as making dents. I use the 40T, which is smaller, for finishing on fiber that isn't firming up or becoming smooth (usually merino). So if I work with a coarser fiber I use 36, with 38 to finish, but with merino I would use 38, with 40 to finish.

I also use a multi-needle tool for the projects. Ones similar to those pictured right are available in most stores that sell felting needles. Multi-needle tools come in different shapes and can take different numbers of needles. I usually fill mine with 36T needles and use it to start off larger pieces, such as heads and bodies, which use a lot of fiber.

You can also buy pen-style needle holders, but most of the brands I've seen have been quite expensive.

Shown above are a 38T needle (left) and a 36T needle (the longer needle), alongside a close-up at right showing the barbs.

Below are two multi tools, with both larger (left) and smaller needles.

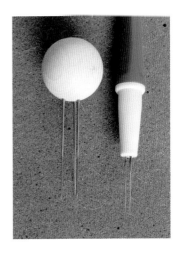

All you need for a basic needle-felting project — fiber, a couple of needle sizes, a multi-needle tool if you have one, and a foam mat.

You can make your own multi-needle tools using an oven-baked clay such as Fimo. I have a two-needle tool that I made six years ago and I still use it every time I felt. Just wrap the ends of the needles in the clay, making sure there is no movement and they are both very straight, then bake according to the manufacturer's instructions.

FIBER

I work with a lot of home-dyed fibers, which means that I don't always know exactly what fiber I'm using. Where I live, in New Zealand, we are lucky to have a lot of wool available to us. I like to work with Corriedale and Romney wools, and I find them especially good for beginners. Both these wools are coarser than merino top, which is super fine. But they are not too coarse, so that your work still has a nice finish.

The fibers you use will depend on local availability, but you should be able to find something similar. With the Internet, of course, you can buy almost anything you like, so if you don't have much available locally get online and buy from the larger online suppliers. They should have information on their fibers and their suitability for felting.

The Character Balls and Lady Linara projects use "core" fiber that is then wrapped with the final color you wish to use. This can be any cheap wool that you have a lot of. Some companies supply a specific fiber that they will call "core," and it is just a cheaper, coarser fiber.

Don't buy anything that is shrink-resistant (super wash), as this fiber is specially designed *not* to felt up when spun into yarn and then thrown in the washing machine. And, of course, we need it to felt up!

My previous book used roving. In this one, I use a lot of fiber batts. You can use them in the same way as other fiber for needle felting, but they don't need to be mixed as much at the start of your work as they are already mixed.

I have found that while batts felt more quickly and are good for sculpting, they don't seem to felt down as firmly as roving fiber does. This is no doubt because the fibers are shorter in a batt and therefore don't tangle down as much as longer roving fibers.

If you are trying a new supplier or fiber, just buy a little, or see if they will send you samples (some places will, especially a local grower who is trying to increase their business). You only need 1¾-oz (50-g) bags to make up to four creatures, so a little fiber goes a long way.

OTHER TOOLS

You will need a surface to work on. This is a matter of choice, but I prefer to use upholstery-grade foam, approximately 2 in (5 cm) thick. The foam in my photos is 8 in (20 cm) square, but use a size that suits you. At home, I use a wooden tray with a piece of foam cut to fit the bottom of it. Leave a few inches each side and you can use the space to stash your tools.

For jointing, I use dental floss. A surprising item, perhaps, but waxed floss is very easy to tie firmly. The knots hold well, it threads easily onto a needle and it's well priced! Just be sure you don't get flavored or other unusual kinds. Waxed ribbon floss is fine too.

You will need needles for sewing and jointing. I use a fine doll needle or a long darning needle. For eye beads, if you don't want to use a beading needle, find long darners or doll needles with small eyes so the beads will fit over them.

Threads come in many different varieties. I like crochet thread (fine) for attaching eye beads and embroidery thread split into three strands for everything else. Collect lots of colors for your stitched details, such as noses and claws, but use black for attaching beads.

Beads in smaller sizes can be hard to source. I like to use ⅛-in (3-mm) round black beads generally, though ³⁄₁₆ inch (4 mm) is good for slightly larger bears, or when I want a more wide-eyed look. Don't use seed beads, as these are not round but have flat sides.

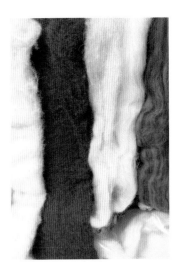

The fiber pictured above, from left: Fiber batts in cream and red/brown, natural Romney roving, Corriedale roving in sky blue and merino top in navy.

CHARACTER BALLS

Our first project! I have designed this project, and those following, to teach you new needle felting skills as you progress through the book. The Character Balls show you how to wind a core, cover it evenly with color and create eyes, lips, and other quirky features.

YOU WILL NEED:

- Core fiber
- Main color fiber
- Fiber for eyes (white, blue, etc)
- Black wool for details
- Felting needles in two grades, and a multi tool (optional)
- Foam mat
- Chopstick or similar
- Scissors

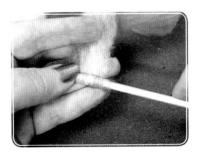

TO BEGIN

Wind your core fiber around the chopstick to create a firm ball, about the size of a tennis ball.

Winding the fiber makes a firm core, as long as you wind fairly tightly. This will then take less time to felt and firm up. (The larger the project, the longer the felting time, so winding your wool will quicken this process.)

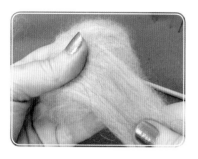

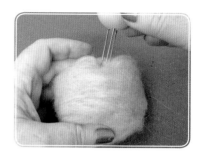

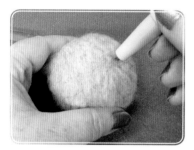

You can use this technique regardless of the final size you are aiming for; even small balls can be done this way. After removing the stick, fluff up the fiber and spread it out a bit so that when you felt the fiber it will be smooth.

Begin needling with your larger needle or multi tool, if you have one. If the core fiber you have used is quite coarse, it will felt up quickly. Finer fibers take longer. Feel free to use a multi tool with finer needles as I have done here to smooth the surface.

Keep felting until the ball feels more solid when it is squeezed, but stop before the ball gets too firm (i.e. before you can't squish it down).

COVERING THE CORE

Take your main color fiber and wrap or lay pieces of it over the core, felting as you go until it is all covered. Do not wrap tightly!

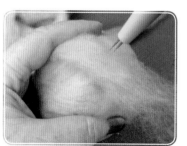

This is a variation on a similar technique that I describe in my previous book *Needle Felting From Basics to Bears*, where I mixed the fiber up into a large "nest" and then wrapped the entire ball, only adding fiber if there were thin spots.

You can work either way to cover a ball with fiber. The method shown here is particularly good if you don't want to use too much fiber, or you feel that you may run out.

Once the main color fiber is felted on with the larger needle, you can change down to a finer needle and work the entire surface until it is smooth.

TIP
You can roll the ball in your hands at any stage to help create its shape or to encourage a smooth surface. Just roll firmly in your palms.

CREATING THE EYES

You are now ready to create the whites of the eyes. For this, take a few pinches of the white fiber and mix it by teasing and pulling it apart with your fingers.

Then place the mixed fiber on your foam mat and needle lightly. Remember to flip it over from time to time, so that the fiber doesn't stick to the surface of the mat.

You may find that you need to use a finer needle for this step. It will depend on your fiber. A large needle will pull too much fiber through and make the piece lose its nice round shape. The finer needle will gently shape it.

Repeat this process three times to create the eyes: first for the whites of eyes, second for the irises and third for the pupils.

If you are having trouble making any of these eye parts round and even, there are a couple of techniques to try.

You can see in the photograph left, that I am pinching the felted fiber between my fingers and carefully needling around the edge of the piece to create an even shape.

Another approach is to create a nice shape on your foam mat by felting on a slight angle as you work around the edge (also shown left). Then flip the fiber and work around the edge again.

Try not to let your pieces get too thick!

Beginning with the white of the eye, when you are happy with the size and shape, put it on the ball. Begin felting to attach.

Starting with the larger needle, felt from the center of the piece working outward. Do not focus on the edges until you are happy that the piece is securely felted on.

Each piece shrinks as you attach it, so if you felt the edge too soon, the piece shrinks and you will see the edge fibers pulling toward the center.

Work around the edge until it is smooth and even.

Then create the iris. Begin by making it almost as big as the felted white. Remember it will shrink when you attach it.

You can see the difference in the size of the iris in the photos above, where I have shown it next to the white before needling around the edge. It shrinks quite a bit with felting and then again as it is attached.

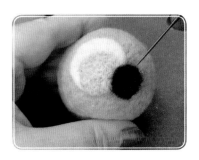

Once the pupil is finished and attached, work over the entire eye with the finer needle to get a smooth surface. You can use your scissors to trim any flyaway hairs.

You can do the eye any way that you like. Different shapes, sizes, colors, and placement of the iris and pupil can create very different looks, and some wonderful expressions. If you want inspiration, just search for "monster art" online.

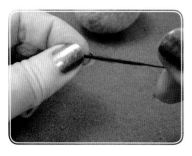

EDGING THE EYES

Once the three pieces of your eye (or eyes) are attached, you are ready to edge the pieces with black fiber. This edging makes a great finish and really defines the eye.

For this, you will take just a few black fibers and gently twist them to form a small rope.

This rope technique can be used for many decorative applications, for example, adding tangled vines to a decorative piece or making initials on a gift.

For the outside of the eye, using the smaller needle, first poke the end of the rope in at the very edge of the eye. Try not to pull the fiber as you work, just hold it in the direction you are going and gently work along the line with your needle. If you pull it too firmly, the fibers won't go into the ball and will instead stay on the surface.

Work all the way around the white of the eye. If you run out of fiber, just lightly felt the end in, trim off any stray fibers and start from there with a new rope.

> ## TIP
> Don't be tempted to felt deeply to attach the end of the rope, as this will create an indentation that will be hard to cover up.

If you have more rope than you need when you get to the end, just hold it firmly and gently pull off the excess, leaving enough to felt the end in. You can go over where you started with the stray fibers to help hide them.

Work over the line a few times with your fine needle to make sure it is well attached, but don't go so deeply that you create a trench!

Repeat the edging for the iris and then trim away any stray fibers with your scissors held flat against the surface of the ball. You won't need to edge the pupil.

So this is your eye done! You can leave it like this or felt little lashes on the side. You could do two eyes like this if you have room.

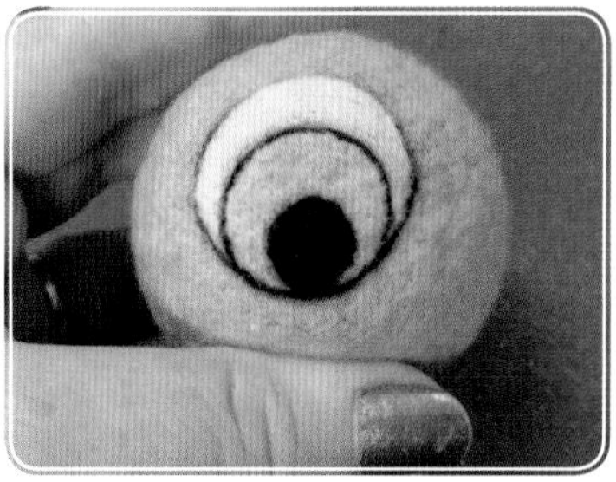

EYELID

Take a small amount of fiber for the eyelid. Mix it well and check for size against the finished eye. Initially, you want it to be enough to cover the entire eye as, of course, it will felt down much smaller.

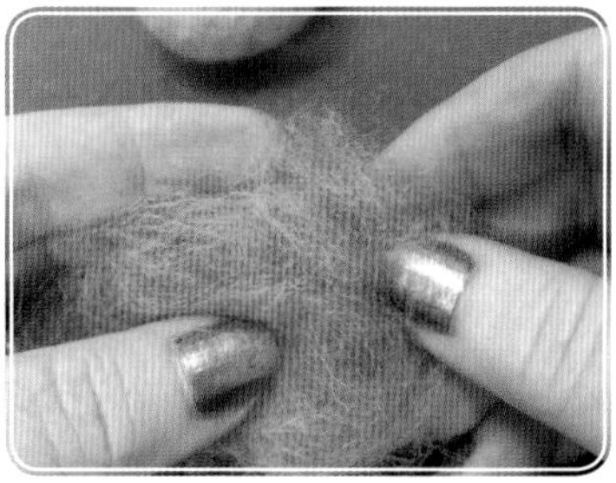

Start working the eyelid by felting it on the foam mat with the larger needle. Be careful not to felt too deeply, as this will take the fibers right through and down into the foam (where they will become embedded and the piece will look hairy). So, felt through the flat piece but not too deep. Remember to flip the piece and felt from both sides.

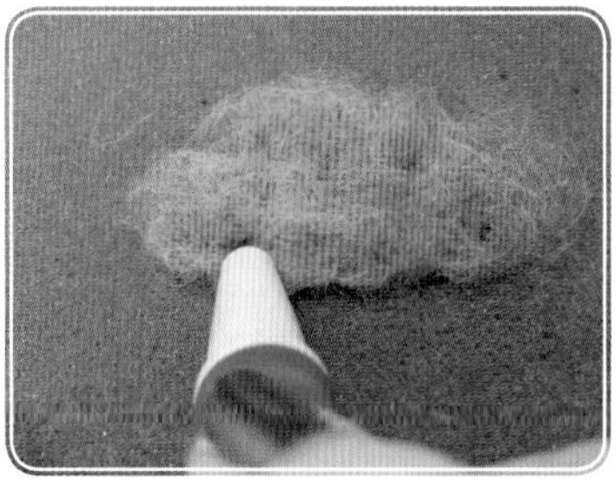

Then, take the fiber in your fingers and create a "side" so that there is a flat area and a curved area. Poke back and forth down the length of this flat area to make it neat and tidy. Work on your foam some more.

You can felt with your needle angled toward the center of your piece, so that the lid will shrink down and be a bit smaller, especially if you feel it is a bit big or thin.

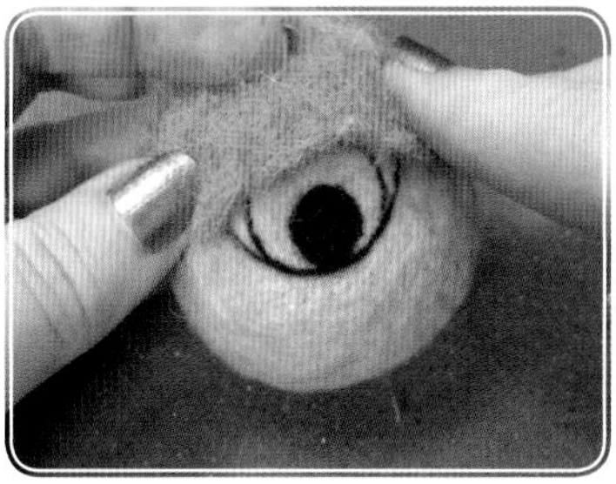

You want the lid to have the same curve as your eye, so you might find that you need to create the shape of the entire lid between your fingers, working all the way around. Just make sure you don't felt until the piece is hard, as it still needs loose fibers to be able to attach it to the ball.

Keep measuring against your eye to make sure you don't go too small; finish with the piece slightly too big. Now we are ready to attach it.

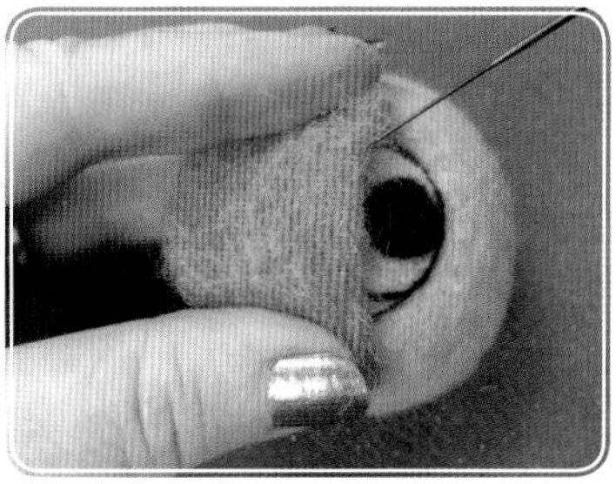

Lay the lid on the eye, matching up the curve at the back of the eye so that the eye is covered and not poking out at the back.

Using the large needle, start felting this lid on with a few pokes all over. If you need your lid to creep back a bit and reveal more of the eye, poke at an angle away from the pupil and toward the back of

the eye. If you work methodically, you will see the lid shrink back as you felt back and forth over it.

Once happy with the position of the eyelid, you can work your edges to keep them nice and clean. Just felt in a line around the shape of the lid and change down to your finer needle to finish off.

EYELASHES

Again, you could stop here, but I decided to add lashes to mine! So, using the rope technique that created the edges of the eye, create a black line under the lash line on the eyelid. I've done it fairly thickly and started with a little "wing" in the black (but I removed this later because I didn't like the effect).

 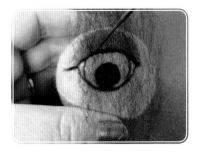 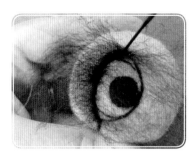

Then, taking the black fiber again, lay it out as you see me doing in the photo. I've just taken pinches and laid them out straight. DO NOT mix this fiber!

Lay the fiber over the eye as pictured above; you may not even need to hold it down, but if you do just use one finger. Now all you need to do is felt along the lash line again with the finer needle. Just work straight along, back and forth, a few times. The fiber will be pulled in as you do this, and the more times you work along the line the more of the fiber you will catch.

I have then lifted the lower fiber up to match in with the upper fiber. You can see that the lash is much thicker now.

Felt along the lash line again to secure, and trim to the length you like. I tend to go long and then trim shorter a few times rather than just cutting straight off in case I go too short!

NOW WE WILL DO A MOUTH!

Taking your lip color, mix and felt on your foam mat just as you did for the eyelid. For this lip shape, you want a longer piece and you will begin to taper the ends into little points as you work.

You can see that I have needled along the edges while holding the piece between my fingers. I often use the finer needle for this as there is not a lot of fiber and the finer needle is more delicate.

Continue to create the mouth shape, and, when you are happy with it, measure it against the ball.

I started attaching the lips by checking the position and then felting deeply with the larger needle in a line to create the part between the lips.

Initially, I just felted back and forth in a line to create that shape. I then worked fairly gingerly around the lips, taking deep pokes at the midpoint to emphasize the indent.

I wanted the lips to be quite three-dimensional, so by working all over rather than straight down, I was able to make them fatter rather than flatter!

Tidy up your edges by working along the lines with your finer needle and you're done!

You can see that by using the techniques learned here you can create lots of different looks.

CURLED-UP CRITTERS

For this project you will need one or two colors, depending on what kind of critter you decide to create. For my project, I have chosen to create a fox and so have used a gorgeous soft tangerine-colored fiber, with white fiber for the tips of the ears and tail. If you were making a cat, you could extend the project by creating stripes on the back, or add long ears and a cotton-tail to make a bunny. These are fun details to experiment with in later projects, but for now we will learn how to make the shape of a sleeping animal, some pointed ears, and a long tail.

YOU WILL NEED:

- ◆ Fiber, in one or two colors
- ◆ Felting needles, large and small (multi tool optional)
- ◆ Foam mat

TO BEGIN

Take a handful of the main color and mix it up well, so that the fibers are lying in all directions and there are no clumps. When working with small amounts of fiber, I just use my fingers to tease it apart. Another good way to do this is to take two flat metal brushes, such as pet brushes, and put the fiber between them. Brush it through a few times.

To gauge the quantity needed for this project, take the fiber and close your hand around it — there shouldn't be much sticking out. A handful of loose fiber can look like quite a lot compared to the size of the final project. Learning how much to use takes some

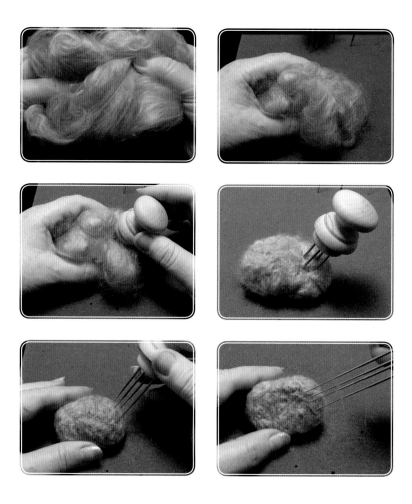

experience. If you want to spend less time on a project, smaller amounts felt up quicker; just don't go too small!

I have started with a multi tool, even though most of the projects in this book don't require you to work with a lot of fiber. However, in the beginning, these tools can be useful to get the fiber compacted more quickly and ready for sculpting.

As the wool felts down, turn the fiber and poke straight in and out with the tool, or a large felting needle. Watch out for your fingers, and aim for a rounded side and a flat side.

If using the multi tool, as it begins to firm up change to the larger of the loose felting needles. Use this needle to refine the shape of your critter, making one side flat and smooth and keeping the other side plump and rounded at each end.

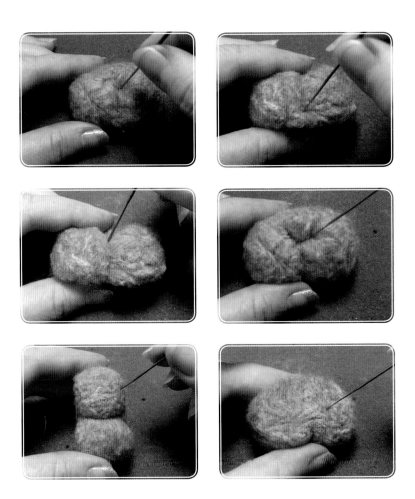

As the shape firms up, run a line down the middle, from about the center of the shape down to the flat edge. Poking along this line will create an indentation. Keep working back and forth until you are happy with the shape, then add the little "Y" shape at the top as in the photo above.

Keep working all over, changing down to the finer needle as your work becomes firmer. Do not let it get too hard, as you need to attach the ears and tail, and wool that is completely felted cannot hold onto the fiber as it is already as felted as it can get. Make sure there is still give when you squeeze your work.

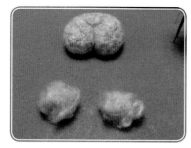
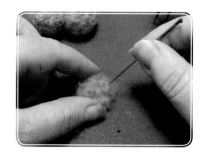

CREATING THE EARS

Taking some fiber (the photograph above indicates the approximate amount), blend and then split into two equal parts. I find that by rolling the two amounts in the fingers of each hand I can more easily determine if they are about the same size.

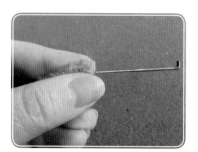

The smaller the amounts of fiber, the harder it is to be sure they are equal, but don't worry too much because as you put everything together things will often look better than they did as small parts.

Work these small balls for a short time with your larger needle before beginning to flatten them on your foam mat.

Next, just work each side, flipping the wool over so that it doesn't stick to the foam.

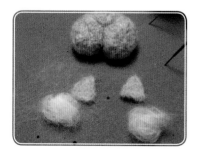

Pinching the piece between your fingers, you can gently create the shape of the ear. This is a delicate procedure so don't rush it, or your fingers will take the toll!

Be sure to leave the lower part of the ear unfelted during the shaping process so that you can use this part to attach to the head.

As you can see, I have created the little pointed ears before adding the white detailing. I have used the finer needle to poke the mixed white fiber a few times before adding it to the ear tips. Don't poke too deeply and just use the finer needle for this process.

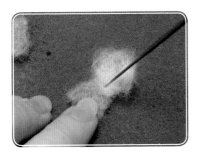

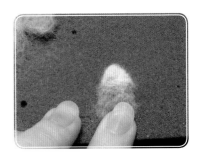

Keep the white piece quite thin, as a thick piece will change the shape of your ear. You can always add a tiny bit more if you can see the ear through the white.

Have you decided which end of the body is the head? If you still aren't sure, try holding the finished ears up against each end to see where they look best. You may want one end to be smaller than the other; it's up to you!

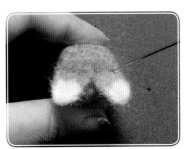

Attaching the ears is simple. Hold them where you want to attach them and then poke with the larger needle back and forth across the ends that you left unfelted.

Once all the fiber has felted in, you can change down to the finer needle to finish off. Make sure they are nice and secure.

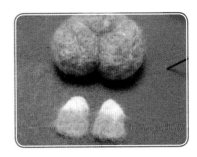

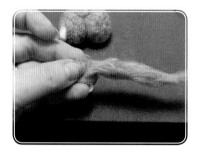 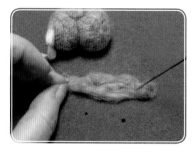 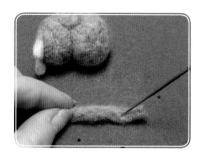

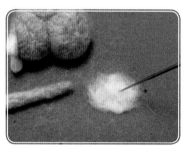

MOVING ONTO THE TAIL

Mix some more fiber and then roll it into a small sausage shape. Work up and down this shape with the larger needle, turning and poking as you go.

Again, leave one end unfelted so that you can attach it to the critter. Hold that end in your fingers as you work as a reminder to leave it until last.

You can add white to the tip of the tail if you wish, working just as you did for the ears. Use the finer needle for this and don't felt too deeply.

Check the length of the tail against your critter body by placing the tip of the tail where you would want it to finish, generally in front of the animal's "face." Then wrap the tail around the body.

If it's way too long, you can always pinch some fiber off the unfelted end. If it's just a little too long, don't worry, it will shorten as you attach it to the body.

If it's too short, you can add a little more onto the unfelted end until you are happy with the length.

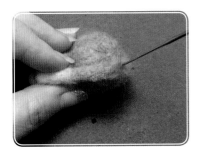 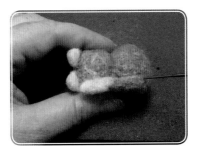

Attach the tail to the body as you did for the ears. Begin by getting the loose end firmly attached with the larger needle. Then work along the tail to the tip with the finer needle until you are happy that it is well attached.

You've done it! I hope you love your little creation. Remember that you can make all sorts of animals this way. Experiment with colors and shapes, and see what you can come up with.

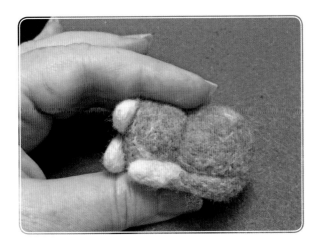

These curled-up critters make great presents. Many people have a favorite animal and because you don't need to add a lot of detail, they do appear quite realistic!

I made another three curled-up critters to show you what else you can do with this project.

TABBY CAT

For this piece you will be learning how to work with batts rather than roving, which was used in the previous projects. This wool is processed differently and is essentially pre-mixed so you don't have to pull it apart as you do for roving. The fibers already lie in different directions and so they can be felted as they are. The fiber I have used here, and recommend, is from Living Felt and is available online worldwide. They also have a great range of felting needles and the fibers come in a wonderful array of colors.

YOU WILL NEED:

- Fiber, in 3 or 4 colors
- Skewer, chopstick or similar
- Eye beads
- Black crochet thread for eyes
- Floss for jointing
- Large and small felting needles
- Long sewing needle for jointing
- Foam mat

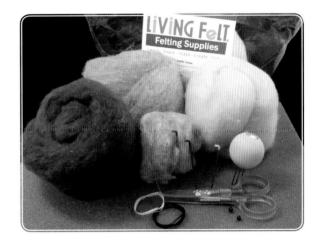

TO BEGIN

Working with batts can make judging how much fiber you need easier. If you pull off pieces of the same size, you can see they will create a similar-sized piece. Because of this, it is more likely that you will have felted arms and legs that are similar in size to each other — there is a lot less guesswork than if you use roving.

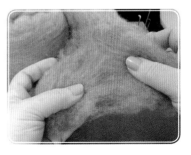

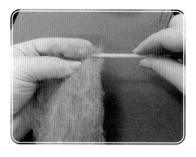
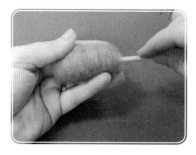

Pulling off a length of roving can be a bit hit and miss for small projects like these. If you have the room on your workspace to lay them out and still work, you can pull off pieces for *all* the parts you will need. This gives you the ability to judge relative sizes, with less for the arms than the legs, and more for the body than for the head, etc. This can be done with roving, but it is harder for newbies.

Take a chunk of fiber for the head and wind it firmly around the skewer. Using skewers in this way means that the fiber will be quicker to felt. Because it is already in a fairly firm ball before you start needle felting, less work is needed.

Don't worry about the amount too much as you can always wind a bit more on. Use the photographs as a rough guide to how big you want the ball to be.

Roll the fiber on the skewer firmly, but not so tight as to flatten and stretch the fiber. You should be able to pull it off the skewer with little effort.

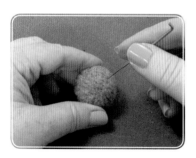

Begin using your larger or heavier grade needle to start felting, poking and turning the fiber to keep the shape round.

Remember that you can roll the fiber in your palms to help keep its round shape.

Once you are happy that the head is moderately firm and even, you repeat this process to create the two much smaller balls in your second color that make up the face of the tabby cat.

  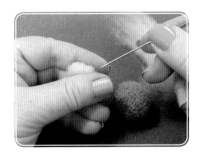

Judging the size of these balls is often tricky. When creating this piece, I found that I had made these balls too small for the head. But I will show you how I fixed this!

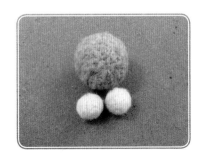

A QUICK FIX

Putting the three balls together I could see that the head was going to be too small (below left). So I took another chunk of fiber and layered it onto the finished ball. With batts you can easily just add another piece and it's seamless compared to roving, where, if you haven't mixed it really well, you can still see the added fibers. I then felted it all over, as evenly as possible, to make the head bigger. You can do this with any piece as many times as you need to.

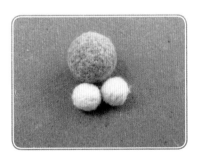 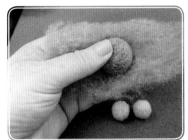

 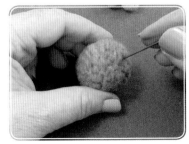 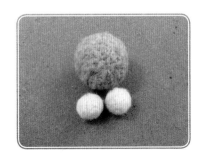

ATTACHING THE CHEEKS

Once you are happy with these three pieces, you can attach the smaller ones to the larger one.

You will want them to be below the center of the head so that they create a forehead. To do this, I hold both balls where I want them to sit and felt deeply with my larger needle. If it is easier for you to do one at a time, that's fine. You should find that a few deep pokes will attach one of the balls, and then you can do the same with the second. In this way, you can check that you are happy with the placement before continuing.

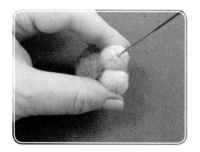

Only when you are sure of their position, felt each ball firmly in place and then work on the entire piece, changing down to your finer needle as you go. You can use your fingers to shape the piece too, for example, pushing the back of the head up if the cheeks are sitting too high on the head.

Once you are happy with the attachment and shape, you will add the chin and the nose. For this reason, you don't want to felt the head and cheeks until the surface is super hard, as then you will not be able to add more pieces to the face.

MAKING THE CHIN AND NOSE

Take two small amounts of fiber and roll them in your fingers to create small balls. Use the photo at right to help you to judge how much fiber to use.

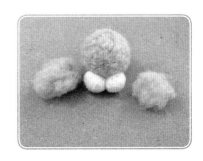

Less is more when creating these smaller features. You can always add another pinch of fiber if the chin and nose aren't big enough once attached. Remember that they do get smaller as you attach them.

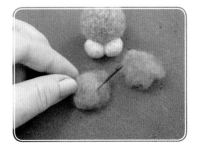

Prefelt the two small pieces a little on your foam mat before attaching one below and one above the two balls that will become the cheeks. Needle them from different angles to help them attach to the cheeks as well as the head, as you don't want any gaps.

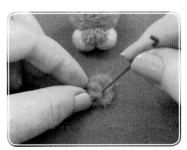

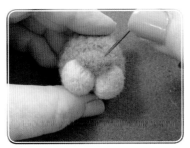

After you have added these, take a little of the pink fiber, or whatever color you have decided to use for your nose, and gently felt it with your finer needle into a little triangle. The idea is that this will cover the end of the piece you just attached for your nose, so use that shape as a guide for how big you need to make this piece. Again, bear in mind that it will shrink a little as it is felted in place, so make it slightly bigger than the space it is going to fill.

Gently felt and shape this piece as you attach it. You can do this entire step with your finer needle, as when you are working with small amounts of fiber the larger needle leaves big holes and is too much for the fine detail we are creating. Work along the edges of the pieces to keep their lines straight.

You will then poke to create little nostrils. Just keep poking in one place with your needle to make these little indents (see photos below).

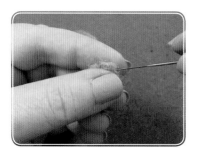

MAKING THE EARS

Take two large pinches of the main color fiber and lay them flat on your foam. With the large needle, felt two lines like the top of a triangle. Then felt back and forth a few times along these lines. Fold the fiber down over the lines into the center of the ear. The fiber will stay attached to the foam mat for the moment to help you create this shape, so don't pull it off just yet.

Felt over the top of the piece a few times to smooth any loose fibers down. Now you can pull the ear off the foam and flip it over.

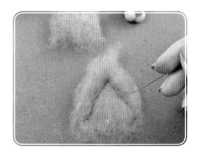

Keep felting both sides this way. Then shape the ear further by pinching the piece between your fingers and felting along the edges. This will help to shrink and thicken the piece. You may find it easier to work both ears at the same time, alternating steps to help them stay the same size and shape.

Don't felt along the bottom of the triangle. This will be where you attach the ears to the head, so you need to leave that edge loose.

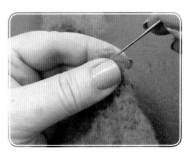

Once you are happy with the ears, bearing in mind that they will change a little as you add them onto the head, it's time to attach them.

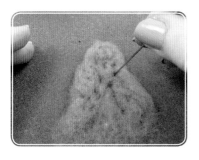
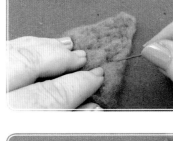

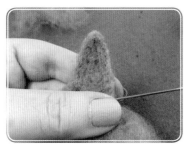
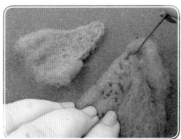

ATTACHING THE EARS

TIP

You may be tempted to add a second color inside the ear. I wouldn't recommend this, as the color will be pulled through by the needles as you attach it. This creates a colored fuzz on the back of the ear. Pieces like these can be darkened once attached using pens or pencils to create shading.

Take both ears and hold them onto the head where you think they should sit. Look at them from the front, as in the photos, to check that you are happy with their placement.

Once the placement is confirmed, remove one ear, ensuring the remaining ear doesn't move as you tack it on with a few pokes from your larger needle. Do the same with the other ear, checking the placement and then tacking it on with the larger needle. If you are happy with how they look, carry on needling. But if they don't look right, you can pull them off and try again.

You can use your larger needle for a while, but if the piece is becoming quite firm, change down to your finer needle. You want to felt the loose ear fibers evenly over the back of the head, working up the back of the ear to the point where it no longer touches the head. Work over all angles to ensure it is well attached.

When I was doing this project, after attaching my ears I noticed what a cute critter this would have made with downward-facing ears. You can see how it looks in the photo below. Does it look cute to you too?

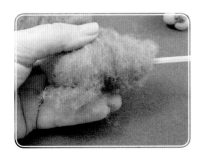  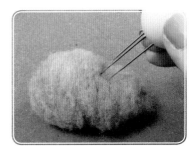

MAKING THE BODY

For this section, take a larger chunk of fiber than you did for the head and wind it onto your skewer. This time, however, you want to have a little more fiber at one end to create a "bottom." It should resemble an egg shape as you begin, but you will refine this shape a little as you work.

Poking and turning with the larger needle (or multi tool), keep working to create a long egg shape. If the neck is too thin or flat sit the "egg" upright and, holding the neck between your fingers, felt down into the body a few times. This should fatten up the end. Just be sure not to poke in the same spot each time or you will make a big dent and the neck will be uneven.

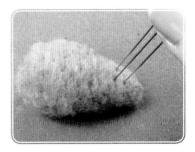

To plump up the bottom, hold the piece by the neck as it lies on your foam mat with the bottom facing the hand you are needling with. Poke into the bottom with the needle angled toward the neck and downward. Felt all around the area and then turn and repeat. You should find that this rounds up the bottom nicely (just watch out for your fingers!).

This is the same method that you used for fattening up the neck, but if you hold the body in the same way that you did for the neck, you will definitely poke your hand so it's safer to do this on the foam mat.

Keep working until the body is fairly firm. Then change down to your finer needle, and work until the surface is smooth.

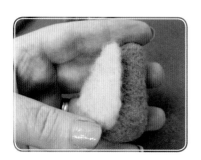

MAKING A COLORED BELLY

Next you are going to create a colored belly for your cat.

Take a pinch of fiber in the desired color that is longer than the body, and on your foam mat start felting the shape you want.

You can do this in the same way that you did the ears if you wish. That is by felting an oval line around the edge of the fiber, and then folding the wispy pieces over and felting them down a little as you move around the edge.

Measure the belly piece against the body as you go. You are aiming to have it longer than the body, measuring from the neck to under the bottom as it will shrink when it is felted on.

Attach by felting the middle of the piece first, and working outward to the edges. Work all over evenly. You will see that there are still little holes visible, and you can either keep working with your finer needle, or, if you are happy with it as it is, rub over the surface firmly with your fingernail. This will roughen it up a little, and make the holes less visible.

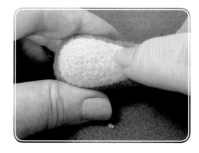

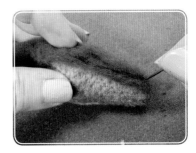

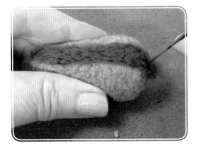
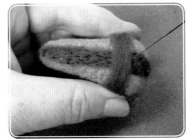
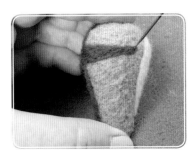

MAKING STRIPES

Now you are going to add the stripes. To do this, take a pinch of fiber and mix it a little. You only want a small amount, and as you can see in the pictures, I have laid this stripe down the center of the back.

Begin needling this piece with your finer needle until the surface is even and you are happy with the shape. We will work on this again once all the stripes are added, so don't worry too much about the surface for now.

Taking smaller amounts of fiber, you can then work the stripes that go around the body. You will have longer ones working up to shorter ones as you go from the bottom to the neck. Lay them directly over the center back stripe, finishing just a bit longer than you want them to be on the belly side as they will, of course, shrink. I have tapered the ends to make a point on each one.

As you create your stripes, you can pull off pieces of fiber if there is too much. I usually pull it from the pointy end before I needle it down.

How many stripes you want to add is up to you, and also depends on how large your body is!

To finish, lay another piece of fiber over the center stripe and felt it in. This hides the horizontal lines, as I didn't like how they looked.

You can now felt all over until you are happy with your stripes. Again, you can rub the surface with your nail when it is firm to smooth it and to minimize any holes.

Next, you will add stripes to the head, working in the same way as for the back. You will need to figure out the placement for your stripes depending on your particular head size and shape, and where the ears sit.

Your center stripe will go up the back of the head and down the forehead, ending in a point between the eyes.

I've managed to fit two stripes below the ears, and then added another two coming from the ears down the face. How many you add will depend on the size of your head. Again, I have covered the center back stripe and felted all over to make sure it is all smooth.

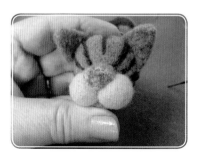

 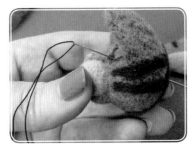 

ATTACHING THE EYES

The next step is to make the eye sockets. This is done by felting in one place to create a dent. Before you start, you may want to experiment with eye placement using a couple of sewing pins and your eye beads. You can put them in various places to see where you like them best, then create the sockets.

It is easiest to make the sockets with your larger needle, but this will depend on how firm your cat's head is. On a very firm head you may need to use the larger needle to get a dent. If the head is softer, the large needle may leave too big a dent.

Remember that you don't use knots in needle felting (except for jointing), so the thread will be anchored by passing it through the head two or three times. Test how well it is anchored by pulling on the thread to see if it is firm. You want the thread to finish coming out at the eye socket.

Add the bead and take the needle into the head at the socket, coming out at the back of the head. Remember to now go back into the head in the same place that you came out to reduce the appearance of stitches in the head. Take the needle through and out the second socket. Then add the second bead, and head back into the socket with your needle, coming out at the back of the head again.

You can make a few passes with your needle back and forth through the back of the head, going in where you came out and keeping these stitches at the back of the head so you don't have stitches on the cat's face. Once you are happy with the eyes, you can cut your thread under tension.

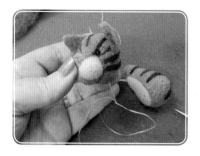

ATTACHING THE BODY AND HEAD

Take the dental floss and cut a 12–16-inch length (30–40 cm). (I measure this by taking the thread in my hand and running it toward my elbow. Cutting it at this length always means I have enough.) Thread the floss onto your needle. It is used as a single strand, so only take the first 2 inches (5 cm) through. If you press this tail against the thread next to it with your fingers it will stop it slipping straight off the needle again.

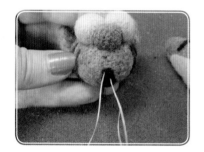

Take the needle through the head from where the neck will be attached and out the top of the head, leaving a tail of about 4 inches (10 cm). Go back into the head where you just came out, but this time come out next to the tail you have left.

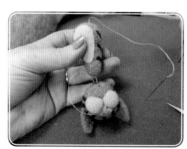

Entering the body at the neck, take the needle down and out at the bottom of the body. Go back in just as you did for the head, but this time you can take a stitch if you wish as it won't be seen and will ensure the joint is firm. Now you will have all your threads at the neck and ready to tie.

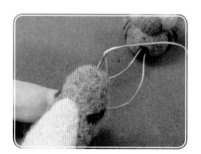

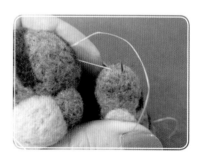

I like to tie it off twice to ensure the pieces will never be at risk of separating. So firmly tie half of a knot, check that you are happy with how the head is sitting, and then tie the rest of the knot.

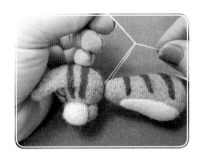

If you aren't happy with how the head is sitting, you can redo the threading and try again.

After the knot is tied, flip the critter over and tie again firmly. Do NOT cut the threads off! Keeping them long, trim them to the same length and thread both back onto your needle.

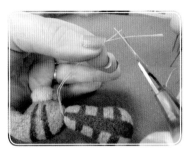

The needle will then enter the neck joint and go down into the body, coming out wherever you like. Then cut the thread as you hold it under tension so that it disappears back into the body.

The head is now attached. If you have a little dimple on the top of the head, you can now fill it by taking the fiber, rolling a small ball without making it too tight, and felting it into the dent with your fine needle. Fluff the ball out a bit so that it doesn't make a line around the edge.

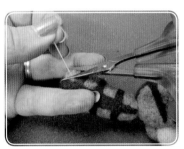

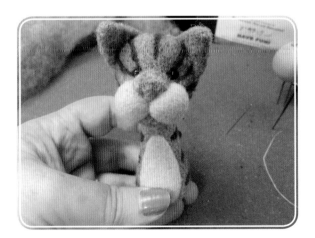

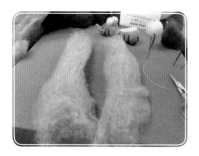

MAKING THE LEGS

To make the legs, take a large amount of fiber and divide it into two equal lengths. Firmly wind the wool around the skewer or chopstick, making sure that you end up with a long shape rather than a round one.

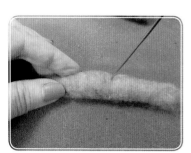

Working with your larger needle, hold one end in your fingers and work the rest of the piece. You want to leave one end loose so that you can add or remove fiber as you go.

Remember to work the needle in at the end so that the leg isn't too flat. You will be attaching the leg to the body from this "hip" end, so it needs to be firm!

I used a spiral needle to felt the legs (see below).

Work down the leg, measuring it next to the body to check the length. At this point, you can add or remove fiber from the loose end to get the length right. Remember though, that you need to allow about one-third to create the foot!

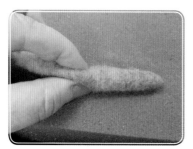

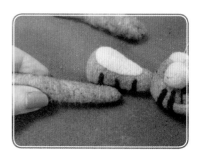

TIP
I used a spiral needle to help speed the process of felting. This needle is amazing: it leaves a smaller hole than the larger needle, but it still felts rapidly.

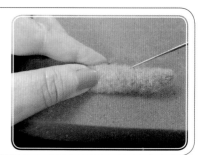

 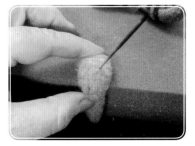 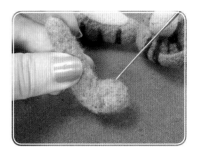

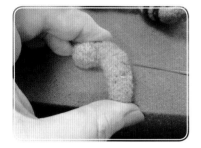 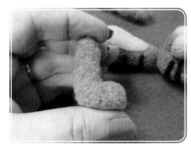 

FEET

Once you are happy with the length of the leg, needle the foot end into a loose ball shape, then fold this over the leg and needle. You can then start to shape the foot.

You can see in the photos above that I flip the leg and then needle the bottom of the foot while holding the leg against the side of my foam mat. Work the foot all over. I tend to shape the heel down to almost an egg shape, while keeping the sole of the foot flat. Once you are happy with the shape, needle all over with your fine needle. Remember to work both feet at the same time.

STRIPES

I decided to do the stripes on the limbs by winding the stripe fiber around the limb. For the most part, this looks like stripes as you can't see both sides of the limb at the same time, especially once it's attached. But you can also add each stripe separately, as you did for the body, if you wish.

> ## TIP
> I start and finish the stripe fiber on the inside of the limb, as this means the ends are hidden.

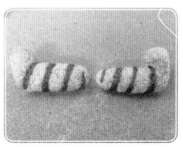

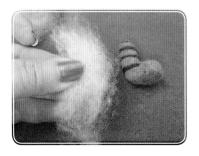

PAW COLORING

I think a kitty looks super cute with "socks," so I've done this for all four limbs of this cat. Of course you don't have to do them, and it may not suit the look you want for your cat. But this is how it's done.

Taking your second color, mix a small amount. You can measure this against the foot, even loosely wrapping it to check you have enough fiber. Be careful not to add too much fiber, unless your foot is smaller than you would like. In which case, you can take this opportunity to make it a little bigger, or even it up with the other.

Mix the fiber, put it on your foam mat and put the foot on top. Then pull the fiber up to cover the top of the foot, needling as you go. Just do this loosely. If you hold fibers tightly against the surface of a felted piece, they won't attach and mix in properly. They will tend to sit on the surface and look tight.

You can see in the photos that I had a "bald" patch that needed more fiber added (below left). So I mixed a little more and added it straight onto the area. When doing this, keep your needling even. Don't concentrate on the "bald" patch, especially the edges — keep them feathery, and they will disappear as you felt.

Once the foot is covered, refine the shape and smooth the surface with your finer needles.

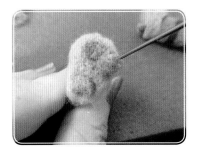

TOE PADS

For the tabby cat, I have made three round pads and a slightly larger oval one, as it looks more cat-like, especially if you can get the little dent into the larger pad. Roll even pinches of fiber between your fingers, and set them out on your foam mat. To check that they are the same size, roll one in each hand and see if they feel the same. Add and remove fiber to even them up (the lower ball will be larger but not by a lot).

Needle these balls a few times with your finer needle to firm them a little before adding them to the foot. If you do this now, they won't turn into flat patches — you want them to be plump. Remember to keep them soft though, or they won't attach!

Add the larger pad first, needling the ball into place, and then working a dent into the lower edge. This is all done with the finer needle and a gentle hand. Sculpting like this takes time, so don't rush. If you work both large pads at the same time, you can go back and forth between them. In this way, if one pad takes a dent really well and the other doesn't you can spend more time on the one that needs it rather than making the dent on the other pad even bigger, leaving you no way to even them up.

Now add the toe pads. Needle the middle one first, and then one on each side. Usually I attach the next pad before the first one is very firmly felted in case I need to adjust anything. Once they are all attached and sitting nicely, finish felting them in place. And you're all done. Hope you are happy with your feet!

> **TIP**
> When you attach them, they can almost overlap, but they will shrink down to fit as you work.

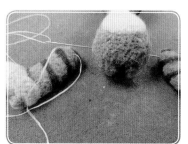

ATTACHING THE LEGS

I like to attach things as I go so that they don't go missing! (Having to re-do pieces would be the worst!) So take your floss and thread one end into the long sewing needle. Enter the leg at the inside hip, coming out the other side of the leg. Then take a small stitch by going back into the leg next to where the thread came out. Pull through just enough to leave a tail for tying off, about 4 inches (10 cm).

Next, enter the body where the leg will attach and go right through to the same place on the other side of the body. Check that you have gone through straight by checking all the angles. Then thread the second leg as you did the first, going back into the body and out the other side.

You should now have your tail and your needle in the same area for tying off. Pull a firm half-knot to check that the legs line up nicely. Finish the knot if you are happy with the placement, keeping the thread pulled tightly as you do to ensure a firm joint.

If you are not happy with the placement of the legs, just pull it all apart and start again.

Remember always to tie two knots. Flip over and tie the second one once you are happy with the placement. DO NOT cut the thread but put it back onto your needle. Then bury it in your work by taking the needle into the body at the joint it is coming out of and taking it out wherever you like. Cut under tension, so that the threads disappear.

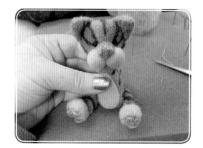

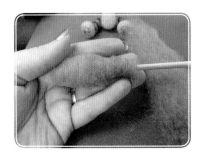
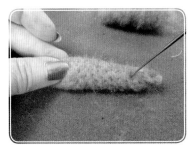
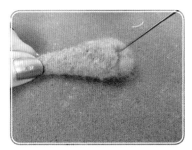

MAKING THE ARMS

Take two lengths of fiber and roll firmly on your skewer to create two sausage shapes. You can add or subtract the fiber at this point if they look the wrong size.

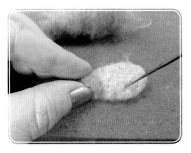

For the tabby cat's "arms," you want to have nice round paws at one end and firm shoulders at the other for attaching to the body. So felt down from the shoulder end with your larger needle. Remember to come in at the end to keep that end solid and work all over the arm as you hold the "paw" end in your fingers.

Check the length of the arm against the body, and once you are happy with it, you can add or subtract length from the paw if you need to. These arms will have two bends in them, so they can be a little longer than you would anticipate as they end up shorter once the bends are in.

Felt the paw into a loose ball shape first, so that it doesn't end up too flat. Once it is holding its shape as a ball, you can start to flatten the paw, felting one side and then the other. Then change down to your finer needle and felt the entire limb, but leave it a little soft as you have more to do yet!

You can either do the paw or the stripes first. I did the stripes first on the legs, but this time I've done the paws first. Add the paw color in the same way as you did for the feet by loosely wrapping the paw in the second color and needling it on with the fine needle. When you are happy with that, add the stripes as before, with the ends finishing on one side — if you can figure out what side will be the inside of each limb!

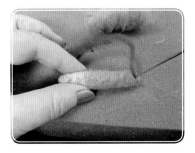

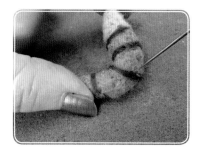
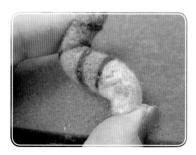

At this stage, you should still have some softness in the limbs as you need to add the bends. The first bend is the "elbow."

Make sure you are holding the paw the right way up so that the elbow bend doesn't go the wrong way. If the paw were flat on your foam, the limb would then go up vertically at the elbow, not across the foam. It can be tricky, so I hope this helps!

Holding with the bend in place, felt a few times with your larger needle to get it to hold the shape. Then continue with the finer needle. Do this for both arms.

The next bend creates the "wrist." So do the same thing as you did for the elbow: put the bend in and then needle until it's holding. Finish by felting all over with your finer needle until the surface is smooth and even!

Joint in the same way that you did for the legs.

Once the limbs are attached, you can fine-tune the shape and position. Holding the limbs against the body you can needle into shape to get a more specific result. Just don't felt too deeply, and move the limbs regularly so they don't stick to the body.

But wait, there's more!

YOU NEED A TAIL NOW

Wind a small amount of fiber around the skewer to create a thin sausage. You want it to be at least the length of the entire cat, but you can do it whatever length you like. Needle the sausage well, and then add the point and the stripes if you wish, using the same method as for the limbs.

For this piece, you will be leaving one end completely unfelted so that you can attach it to the body. The other end is the tip of the tail. Felt the tail and the tip well, as you want it to be finished when you attach it, unlike the ears, etc., which you can felt further after they are attached.

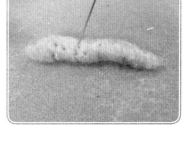

Fluff out the end that you are going to attach to the body so that it will disappear into the body piece, but don't have it so big that it covers your stripes.

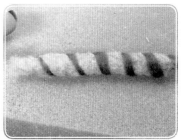

I decided that I wanted the tail to go up my cat's back, so I attached it under the body and pointing upwards This meant that his stripe needed to be put in again to cover that join. This is easily done, and it adds to the strength of the tail, as people tend to pull on the tail when you show them what you have made!

Move the tail around so that you can felt the base from all angles and ensure that it is well attached. I have then added some shaping to my tail by holding it with the curves in it and needling those with my finer needle. These curves will hold, but if they are played with the tail will straighten out. If you want to keep the shape of a piece like this, you could felt over a pipe cleaner. Just make sure the sharp ends of the pipe cleaner are curved in at the top and embedded into the body at the attached end.

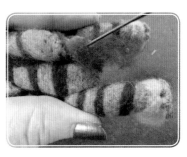

Phew…you're all done! I hope you love your little kitty as much as I love mine!

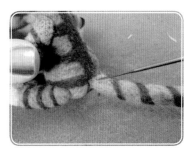

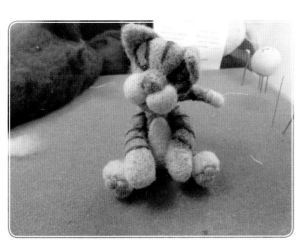

DIZZY DUCK

During this project you will learn how to add weight to your piece, how useful a basic pattern can be, and how to make your work fluffy!

YOU WILL NEED:

- Fiber (batts or roving) in 2 colors of your choice
- Steel shot (smallest size)
- Eye beads
- Black crochet thread for eyes
- Floss
- Felting needles in 2 or 3 grades
- Skewer or chopstick
- Foam mat
- Scissors
- A reverse felting needle

TIP

If you aren't using fiber batts you can still do these projects, you just need to mix the fiber yourself. See page 23 for instructions on how to do this.

BEGIN WITH THE HEAD

Take enough fiber for the head and use the skewer to wind it into a ball. The photos show you how to do this. Even though the fiber comes off the skewer as a long shape, you can felt it into a ball by coming in on each end with your needle and working evenly around the piece to keep it round.

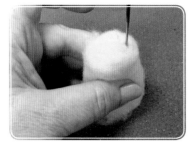

Don't forget that you can also roll it firmly in your palms as you work it to help keep the shape. Felt the head until it is firm but not hard.

ADDING THE BEAK

Take the fiber you have chosen for the beak and make a small oval shape. Felt it on your foam mat for a few moments. Once it is holding its shape, attach it to the head. Work around the base of the beak to get a good attachment to the head.

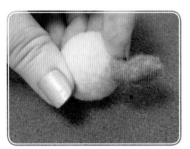

When firmly attached, work over the entire beak briefly before starting to define the shape of the open beak by working a line into the piece. Keep working your needle back and forth along the line to create the shape. You can also press your thumbnail into the line to help define it.

TIP
If this process doesn't work for you, all is not lost! It can be done in two pieces. Just felt a little piece of fiber and attach it under the first one to make the lower "jaw."

 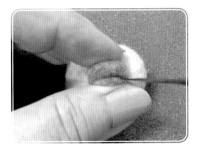 

  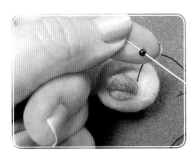

Once you are happy with the beak, you can work the entire piece with your smaller needles to get it nice and smooth.

ATTACHING THE EYES

Decide where you want to attach the eyes. Then take the larger felting needle and begin working in one spot to make the eye socket. Repeat for the other eye.

You can see from the photos that I've done one eye on each side of the beak. But you can put them wherever you think they will look best.

Attach the eye beads with your black thread as shown on page 43.

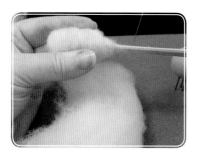 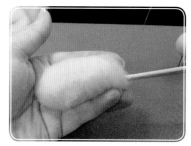 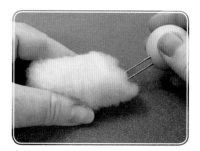

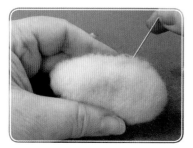 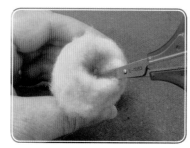 

MAKING THE BODY

Take the fiber for the body and wind it up with your skewer (or mix by hand if you are using roving) and work into shape. This time, you want to create an egg shape initially. So felt the "bottom" end while holding the "neck" end and then reverse to work the "neck" end.

Work the neck end a bit more firmly than the bottom end, as you are going to be shaping the bottom and adding the weight so you don't want it to be too firm at this stage.

While the bottom is still soft, shape it as shown in the photos. Then, create a small dent or hole in the piece so you can add your steel shot. Either use your fingers or scissors, depending on how loose the fiber is. You should be able to push the shot in with your fingertip. The total amount of shot will vary depending on your piece, but it is usually around a teaspoon.

 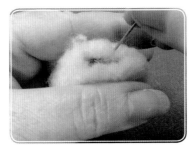 

 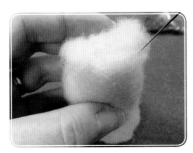 

Pull the fiber up around the shot to create the bottom of the piece. You can add more fiber if needed to fully cover the shot. To do this, felt a small piece on your foam before adding to the body so that it has some thickness to it before you start, Try to keep the edges loose so that it will be a seamless patch. (I added two patches to ensure that the shot was well hidden.)

Once covered, continue to shape your little duck bottom, creating a cute little tail as well.

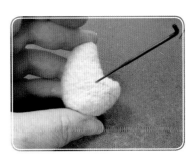

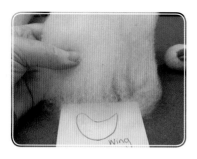 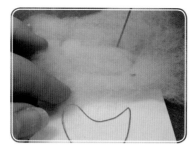 

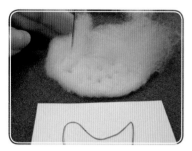

WINGS

Now you can make a pattern for your duck's wings. You can draw your own, as you will be able to ensure that they will be a good size for the piece you have already created. Or you can use the photos as a rough guide; but they may be too big or too small depending on the body size of your duck.

To create the wings, take a small amount of fiber. Then, using your needle almost like a pen, felt in and out around the edges to make an outline of the shape you want on your foam mat. Remember to make your wings bigger than the final size you need as they will shrink down and thicken as you felt.

Note: If you are using roving rather than batting, you will need to mix your fiber before this step. Try not to use too much fiber or the wing will be very thick.

After you have the shape outlined, fold any loose fiber up and onto the wing to create a nice edge. Felt this loose fiber lightly with the large needle. Then continue around the piece until all of it has been lightly felted into place before lifting it carefully off the foam mat and working the other side.

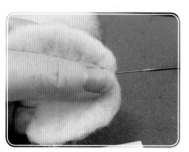

You may find it easier to start the second wing at this point, as this will help to keep them the same size and shape, but start whenever you are ready.

As you can see in the photo, you will need to hold the wing in your fingers and work around the edges (still with the larger needle), to help shrink the shape and define the wing. If you are working both wings at the same time, you can go back and forth between them during this stage and compare for size.

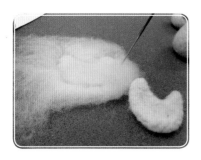 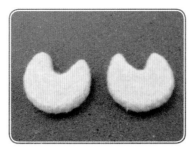 

As the wings firm up, remember to change to the finer needle to get them smooth and solid.

One end of the wing will be more rounded — this will be the "shoulder"; and the other will be pointed — this will be the tip of the wing.

LEGS

When making arms and legs on any critter or doll it is always best to make both of them at the same time. It is much easier to keep them the same size and shape if you do this.

With this in mind, wind the fiber for the legs to create two long shapes. You will initially be working only at one end. This will be the "hip" end of the leg, so hold the foot in your fingers as you work.

Felt these pieces to create the length you would like your legs to be — just be sure to make them both the same length! Before making the feet, ensure that both foot ends have about the same amount of fiber so that the feet will be roughly the same size.

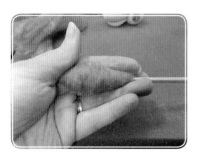 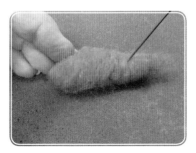 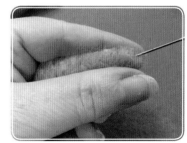

 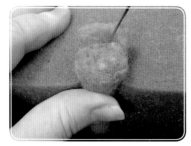 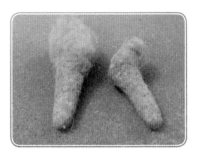

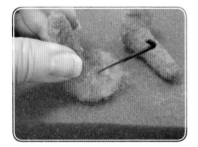 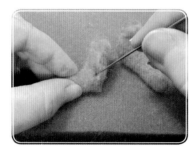 

Fold the loose foot piece back over the leg and felt into the "heel" for a few moments.

You can see in the photograph (above center) that I placed the foot on the foam mat with the leg down the side of the square so that I could concentrate on the bottom of the foot without getting my fingers in the way. Continue to felt in this way to create a flat surface, but don't let it get too thin and wide.

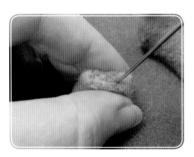

Then work the sides by gently poking from the heel up on both sides of the foot. You will be creating almost a triangle shape with the wider, rounded end where the "toes" would be.

Carefully make little indentations either side of the middle "toe." You may need to change down to your finer needle at this point.

Keep working all over the foot, shaping and comparing the two feet to get them the same size and shape. Pinching the foot between your fingers can help to more easily shape the webbed feet.

Remember, if you aren't happy with the finished legs you can always make another pair. Better to waste a little fiber than to be unhappy with your new friend!

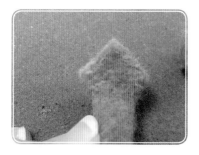

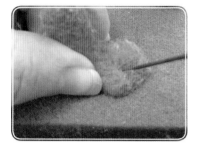

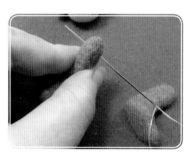

Work all over with the finer needle to get the legs and feet nice and firm. You can see in the photos how long my legs were at the beginning and how much they compacted down during this stage.

I wanted them firmer and shorter, so I worked the needle at an angle to help achieve this. I also held the legs while pushing them shorter as I felted. This speeds up the process, but watch out for your fingers. Making the legs a little flatter helps them to sit nicely against the body, too.

Joint the wings and legs just as you did for the Tabby Cat's legs and arms (see page 50).

At this point, you can create a little belly button by felting in one place with the larger needle, just as you did for the eye sockets.

TIP
If you don't have a reverse felting needle and still want to make your duck fluffy you can use a wire animal brush or similar to brush each piece now *before* you joint the wings to the body. I mention this now, as using a brush after jointing is incredibly hard!

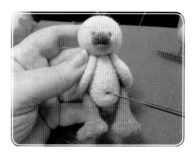

MAKING YOUR DUCK FLUFFY!

The following instructions describe how to use a reverse felting needle to make the duck fluffy. If you don't have one of these, you will need to use a wire brush and make the pieces fluffy *before* you joint them together. If you have neither a brush nor a reverse needle you can use a sewing needle. Firmly scratch the sewing needle across the surface of the finished piece to fluff up the fiber. This gives a more uneven result than the brush and reverse needle, but you can always use the fine needle to poke overly fluffy areas back down.

Take the reverse felting needle and work methodically in rows across your piece so that you don't miss any areas. The reverse needle grabs very quickly, so you don't need to poke deeply, you are just working the surface. Hold the duck firmly so that it is not pulled from your hand or you could break your needle.

I used the reverse needle on the head, tail, belly, and wings to varying degrees. I made the head the most fluffy. Don't worry if some of the fibers look quite long, with handling or a quick rub, it will look evenly fluffy.

I hope you have enjoyed making your own
Dizzy Duck.

ELLE ELEPHANT

This little elephant is created using wool roving. She will teach you a number of new techniques, such as shaping "hoof"-style limbs. These are great for pigs or cows, goats and other hooved animals Also there is more practice sculpting facial shapes, such as cheeks, and, in this case, adding the long trunk. Finally, I'll show you how to create a simple dress to really make your work unique.

YOU WILL NEED:

- Fiber in main color of your elephant (I have used gray natural Corriedale in roving)
- White fiber for tusks, eye whites, and toenails
- Felting needles, large and small (or multi tool, optional)
- Foam mat
- Something to color the cheeks; you can use makeup and an applicator, soft colored pencils or chalks, as I did
- Eye beads
- Black crochet thread or similar for eyes
- Dental floss for jointing
- Fabric for dress
- Fine ribbon or thread to tie dress
- Sewing thread and needle for dress

THE HEAD

Take the amount of wool you would like to use for the head and felt it into a ball with your large needle or multi tool. (You can see roughly how much roving I used in the photos. I have

 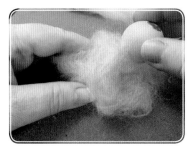 

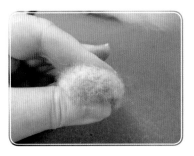

stuffed the wool into my closed hand, with just a little poking out.) Do not felt too long, as you want the head to still be easily squished. You will need to add the cheeks and the trunk onto the head while it is still soft enough.

ADDING THE TRUNK...

Take a small amount of fiber for your trunk. Mix and roll it into a sausage. Use the photos to gauge the size.

Work the fiber for the trunk on your foam mat, but don't forget to keep turning and moving it. This stops the trunk sticking to the surface of the mat. It also prevents foam pieces from the mat breaking off and getting inserted into your work (this can happen as the foam starts to break down from a lot of use!).

Change down to your smaller needle and keep working the trunk until it is firm but not hard, leaving a loose end for attaching it to the head.

Once you are happy with the trunk, fluff up the loose end and attach it to the head with your larger needle. I do this from all angles to ensure a firm and even attachment. Remember not to focus on the edges as you felt, but work the entire surface so that the piece blends in well.

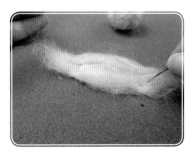 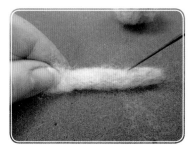 

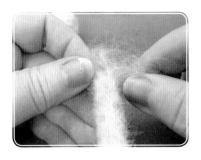

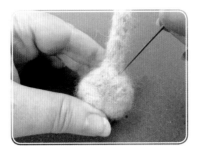

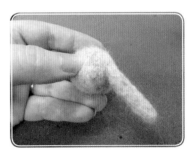

Your trunk is probably sticking straight out at this point, so fold it over a little and needle it to create the angle.

...AND THE CHEEKS

Take two small even amounts of fiber and felt them into small balls until they are about as firm as the head. Then check the placement. I have done the cheeks very close to the trunk, but remember that they will shrink down smaller and be further away from the trunk as you felt them.

Add them on by starting with the larger needle and changing down as you go. Needle the entire surface and don't focus on the edges or they will stand out rather than blending in.

Work the whole face with your finer needle.

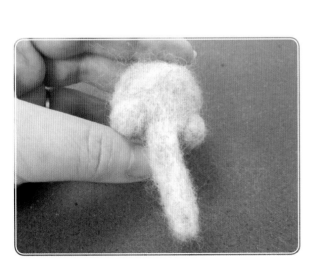

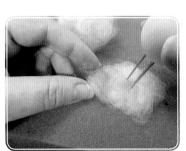

Now to create some detailing on the trunk. I have needled directly into the end of the trunk to create a little dent, and also needled back and forth in little lines across the trunk to create the little indentations you can see in the photograph. Some fibers will do this better than others, and it will depend on how firm the piece is also, but do your best. You can always darken these areas with a soft colored pencil later! (See Denny Dragon, page 91.)

Don't worry too much about felting the back of the head as we still have to add the ears.

THE EARS

Take equal amounts of fiber for the ears. You can see here that I've pulled off one piece of roving and then split it into two before mixing each piece well. This helps to keep them even.

I find felting on the foam mat with a multi tool helps to create a flat piece, but you can work with a single needle equally as well. Again, remember to flip over regularly to prevent sticking.

It's up to you what shape you make your ears. You may choose to go completely round or have a search online to get an idea of shapes (I've shown you my shape here). The most important thing is to get the ears as similar in size and shape as you can. You can even go quite big, as long as the area for attaching isn't too big for the back of the head. I have tapered off the ear to a narrow loose edge so there is room to attach.

Holding the ear, work between your fingers to create a nice edge. Keep needling, and change down to your finer needle as you go. You want to have the ears finished and with an even, smooth surface before you add them to the head, as that is the last step.

Work both ears at the same time, moving back and forth between them to help keep them similar in size and shape.

Check the ear placement and, when you are ready, attach the ears with your larger needle. Then felt the surface all over with your finer needle until it is smooth. You will felt about a quarter of the ear onto the head when attaching.

THE REST OF THE FACE

Taking your larger needle, make indentations for the eyes.

Remember, you can check eye placement by putting a pin through each eye bead and testing positions on the head.

Make both indents and then thread your sewing needle with black thread, roughly 16 inches (40 cm) long. (Don't knot the end, as knots are not used in needle felting, except for jointing. Your thread will be anchored by passing through the head two or three times.)

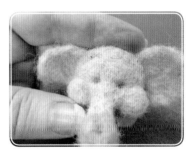

Take your needle in at the socket, and go straight through the head, coming out at the back. Pull the thread through until the very end disappears into the socket. Then take the needle back into the head where the thread is currently coming out; this time the needle will come out at the socket. Repeat this step another two times, stopping with the needle and thread exiting the socket. A pull on the thread will tell you if it is firm or not. Remember to go back into the head in the same place that you came out to reduce the appearance of stitches at the back of the head.

Add your bead and take the needle back into the socket and through, coming out at the back of the head. Then go back through the head, coming out at the second socket. Add the second bead, and head back into the socket with your needle. Pull firmly; the eyes should settle into the socket a little.

Then make a few passes with your needle back and forth through the back of the head, going in where you came out and keeping the needle at the back of the head so you don't do stitches on his face. (See page 43 of the Tabby Cat project for further photos.) Once you are happy that everything is firm, you can cut your thread under tension.

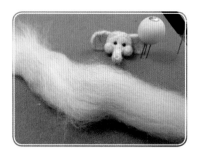
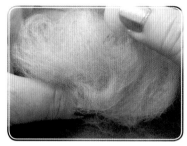
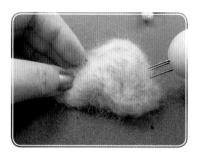

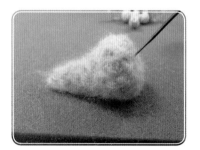

MAKING THE BODY

Take the fiber for the elephant's body and mix well. Felt it into the usual egg shape, starting with the larger needle and switching to the smaller needle as it firms up so that you have a firm, smooth shape. Then attach the head and body using the dental floss. (For instructions on jointing head, body and limbs see the Tabby Cat project on pages 44 for the head and 50 for the limbs).

MAKING THE LIMBS

For this project I thought it would be a good idea to show you the amounts of fiber used for the limbs. Take one amount of fiber for the legs and one for the arms, ensuring the amount for the legs is a little more than the arms, as they will be longer. Then split each piece of fiber equally into two, so you have four limbs. Mix well before rolling into the sausage shapes you see in the photograph left. The arms are the shorter pieces at the top of the photo. In this way, you won't have to guess how much you used for one set of limbs and then try to use more or less than that when you have felted one set and are starting the other. And you can needle all four limbs alternately so they are a similar shape and keep true to the size you want.

 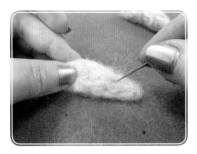 

The limbs are worked in a similar way to the previous paw-style arms, with one end left soft and the other felted into a thick point, nice and firm for attaching. But this time, after felting the paw end into a rough ball, it will be poked from the end to create a flat area. You can see in the photograph that I am holding the limb in my fingers and gently felting the end. *Do not go too deeply as you are likely to get your fingers!* You can do this on the foam mat as well if you find that easier, just keep turning the limb as you go to keep it even.

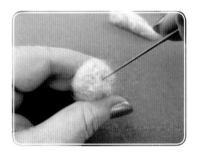

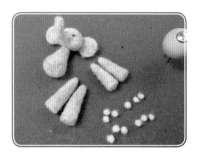  

Once you have made all four limbs, you can start rolling your white fiber into tiny balls for the nails. I have done three for each foot, but you could do four if they fit. Make the balls as similar as possible. Only a very tiny amount of fiber is needed for each nail, and once you have rolled a few you will get a feel for how much you need.

Hold each ball in your fingers and give it a few pokes with your fine needle. Or you can do this on your foam mat, but don't poke too deeply or the ball will be very "hairy" when you attach it. A few little pokes will help it to stand out when you attach it so it won't sit too flat.

Attach the nails with your finer needle. The larger one doesn't work for this job as it is too difficult to poke into the fiber and drags too much fiber out through the back of your work, making it fluffy.

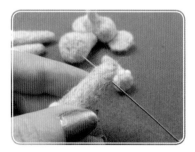

ATTACHING THE LIMBS

See Tabby Cat (page 50) for full instructions on attaching limbs.

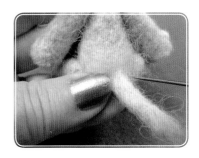

MAKING THE TAIL

A tail is a cute detail to add and it has a practical use in that it can help your creations to sit well and not fall backwards. I sometimes add them to my bears as well, but obviously cows and pigs look super cute with tails just like these ones.

Mix a small amount of fiber and roll it between your fingers. Needle with your smaller needle on the foam mat. Ensure one end is left loose for attaching to the body, and felt the rest until it is smooth and firm. Remember not to poke too deeply. This helps to keep the piece from appearing too hairy.

I wanted my tail to have a hairy little tip, so I used a sewing needle to pull/comb some of the fiber out after felting. You can also do this with a reverse needle.

Check the placement of the tail when the elephant is sitting. There is nothing worse than putting it too low! Tease the fiber to attach and felt all over with your small needle.

At this point, I have also added a little belly button by felting in one spot with my larger needle.

FINISHING TOUCHES

At this point, I decided my elephant needed little pink cheeks. You can create these with any soft powdered color. I had some chalks handy, but powder eye shadows or blush work equally well. You can also gently rub a soft colored pencil, such as a watercolor pencil, over the area.

Less is more with the powders, so just add a tiny bit to start with. You can always add more, but taking it off is pretty hard!

Apply the powder with a makeup sponge or a Q-tip. (See Denny Dragon, page 91, for instructions on how to use colored pencils.)

EYE WHITES

Take tiny amounts of white fiber, roll them in your fingers and use a fine needle to poke them under the eyes. Sometimes this goes really well, and at other times it really doesn't!

Don't poke them too much, and work on both at the same time. It is a case of the smaller the better, so work right up into the eye socket and under the bead so that the white almost disappears. (See page 77 of my first book, *Needle Felting From Basics to Bears*, for more information on eye whites.)

One reason for not felting the eye whites too aggressively is that you can always pull them off if you can't get them even or decide they don't look right. On Elle they almost disappear because of her light coloring.

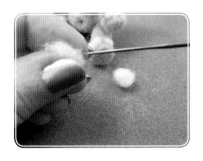 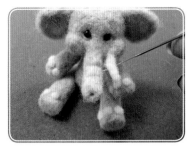 

TIME FOR TUSKS

Take two tiny amounts of white fiber and needle with your smaller needle to create oblong shapes. Make both at the same time, and attach at the same time. Attach them right next to the trunk and work back and forth between them as you poke and attach with your small needle.

Doesn't she look cute?

MAKING A DRESS

This is a very basic dress, and because it's tiny I'm not unpacking my sewing machine and setting it all up for a 2-minute job! If you happen to be blessed with a sewing space and already have one set up I'm sure you will miss this step (and if you have a sewing space you probably already know how to make an amazing little dress!). We are keeping it basic here — anyone can do this!

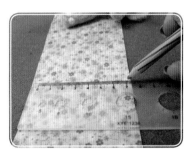

Using a ruler, I have taken a measurement from chin to toe. I will cut my fabric at least this wide and a little more to allow for seams. I decided the length by wrapping the fabric around her very loosely and measuring how long that was, adding a bit for seams, and then cutting. If you wanted to, you could do this with paper first to create a template, then cut the fabric according to your pattern.

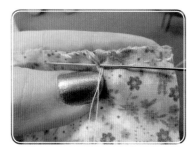

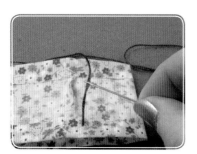

I have then folded the fabric in half, short sides together and right sides together, to create a join or seam that will go down the back of the dress. With a sewing needle and thread, sew tiny stitches down the seam and tie off the thread.

Then hem the top and bottom of the dress by folding the edges and running a row of tiny stitches along these as well. (Before sewing the second hem, I measured the dress on Elle to make sure it was not too long or short for her, as I could make this hem bigger or smaller as needed at this point.)

I want to gather and tie the dress on with a thread so I have used a long piece of matching embroidery cotton (but you could use fine ribbon or any other thread for this). I used my sewing needle, but it was quite a pain as it kept sticking out of the fabric so I would recommend a blunt wool or tapestry needle if you have one, or you can turn the needle around and put the eye into the casing first, just make sure you thread the needle well so it doesn't just fall off as you go.

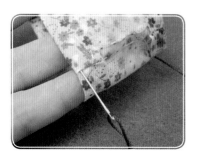

Take the needle into the seam where there is a gap in the sewing, and use the needle to pull the thread through the middle of the hem, coming all the way around and out at the seam again. This should create two ends that you can pull together to tie and gather up the dress.

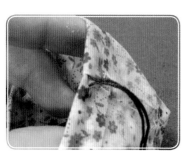

 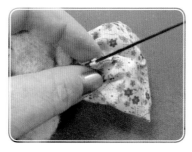 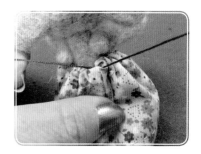

Pop your elephant into the dress (once you have turned it through the right way), pull it up under her arms and then firmly tie. You could do a knot and then a bow if you wanted to make sure it won't come off.

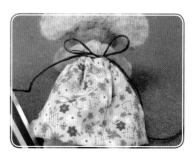

Hey guess what? You're done! I hope you enjoyed making a little elephant with me. As you get more confident with needle felting techniques, there are many ways that you can adapt these instructions to make similar-styled animals you can gift to friends and family.

DENNY DRAGON

I am so pleased with how this project came out. Denny was created using batts for his green coloring and roving for the white. This project teaches you how to sculpt your pieces before they become too firm, and how you can build up your piece with the shapes and details you want. I will also show you how to add shading to your work. I do hope you enjoy creating your own dragon!

YOU WILL NEED:

- Felting needles, in two or three sizes
- Multi tool, if you have one
- Foam mat to work on
- Fiber in at least two colors
- Eye beads
- Black crochet tread for eyes
- Dental floss for jointing
- Long sewing needle
- Watercolor pencil or other similar soft-leaded pencil in dark complementary color

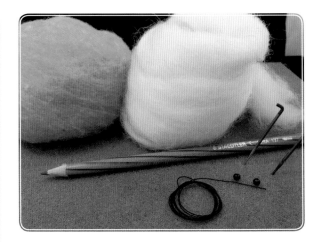

MAKING THE HEAD

Begin by taking enough fiber for the head and creating a soft ball. Remember that the amount of fiber for a head is roughly the amount you can fit into your closed fist. So pull some fiber, and close your hand around it. Is there a lot of room or are you struggling to poke all the extra bits in? If the first is true, then you need more fiber; if the second is true, then you may have too much.

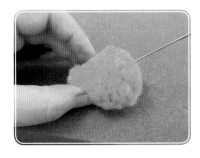

Work with your larger needle until the ball holds together but is still soft. Then you can start shaping it from a ball into a more egg-like shape.

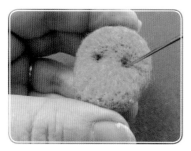

You will see that the snout shape is achieved by creating a flatter end with a little turn up. Don't work the piece until it is hard, as you now need to create the mouth.

Following the photos, you can see that I have taken the larger needle and worked a line around the edge of the muzzle, creating a mouth. Work this line back and forth a few times, changing down to the finer needle as you go.

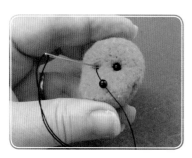

Work slowly and don't needle the top lip too much or it will not be very prominent (it needs to slightly overhang the bottom jaw). If you feel the top jaw has disappeared and you want to try adding to it, go to the step for making the sculpted brows (below), as you can use the same technique to add more fiber here.

Next, choose where you will put your eyes. Remember that you can put your beads on a pin and try out various positions first. Make your eye sockets by needling in one place with the larger needle to create an indent. Then thread and sew your eyes into place just as we have with our other projects (see page 43).

CREATING SCULPTED BROWS

This is a great technique for making an addition with a smooth edge. You might need to do this to build up sculptural elements in any number of projects, so it is a technique that is well worth learning. For this project we are making two brows.

Take two small amounts of fiber. If you are using roving, mix your fiber as you normally would before the next step.

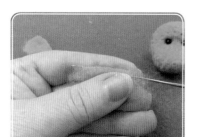

 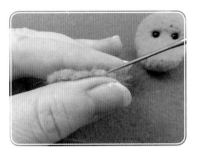 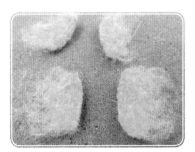

Using the needle to create a fold line, fold the fiber over as shown and lightly needle. You may have to do this step twice, as I have. It will depend on how thick it is after the first fold. Remember that you can try making these a few times before the finished pieces are attached.

If they turn out too small or too thick, just make some more until you are happy with them. You will then need a second set of two for the nostrils, so the odds are that you can mix and match to get two sets of a similar size.

Make these pieces a little bigger and longer than you want in the finished piece as there will be shrinkage as you needle.

Due to the small size of these pieces, work with the finer needle, keeping one long edge and the two short sides loose and unfelted. Only the front edge needs to be smooth and finished as the rest will be attached to the dragon.

To attach the brows, start between the eyes and slightly down onto the snout. Hold the piece gently and poke the end into place. Curve the piece around the eye bead and gently needle around the eye. Then stop and check that you are happy with placement. You can loosely attach the other brow at this stage if you want to work them both at the same time.

Felt inside, between the bead and the brow, and then outside, along the top curve of the brow. Don't work the edge until you are happy with the attachment and shape.

In the two photos at right, one shows the brows fairly well attached, and the other shows how they look after they have been needled for a while with the fine needle. This firms them and shrinks them down to a size I like.

MAKING THE NOSTRILS

Then do the same as you did with the brows to attach the nostrils. This can be a bit fiddly, as you want to hold them in the required shape with one hand while you gently needle with the other.

Don't be afraid to pull them off and try again if the placement isn't equal after you start. Work the inside and outside of the nostril as you place them, as you did for the brows. Once you are happy with the placement, work all over with the fine needle. Work back and forth between the two, so that they stay the same size and shape.

It is especially important with these pieces to fluff the edges out when you are placing them, so that they disappear into the face without leaving any lines or lumps. Again, you can see my before and after photos.

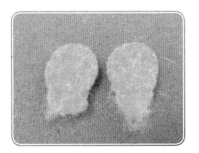

MAKING THE EARS

Create two round ears. For this project, don't make them too small as they will be folded over, or too thick, as folding thick ears is more difficult. As always, there is a loose edge of fiber where the

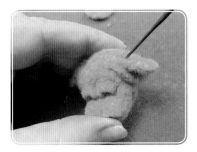

ears will be attached. Make them smooth and "finished" at this stage, as they will only be attached, and not refined.

Pinch the edges of the ear together and needle into place. Remember to do both with a few pokes initially, and then check placement before continuing.

SPIKES

Taking your complementary color, roll some tiny balls from pinches of fiber. You can see that these aren't very big, and you only need three or four, depending on the size of your dragon's head and how close you want the spikes to be.

Carefully needle each ball between your fingers with the finer needle. It will firm up after a few pokes. Then, holding onto the head, needle each ball into place. Once the ball is attached, pinch it with your fingers and gently needle the fiber between them. This helps to create more of a pointed shape. Move your fingers around the "spike" as you poke between them so that you felt the entire piece.

Do this for a few balls, but remember to leave room for attaching the head to the body.

  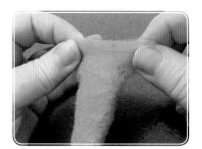

MAKING THE BODY AND TAIL

Initially, you will be creating the same egg shape that you have done for the earlier projects (see Tabby Cat, page 39). So take your fiber, and either mix or roll to create an egg shaped body. But don't felt too firmly at this stage.

Next, take a similar amount of fiber to create the tail. For the tail, roll the fiber into a sausage shape. Then felt the tail, leaving one end unfelted for attachment.

When both pieces are firm but not hard, fluff out the tail fibers and attach the tail to the body, needling all over to hide the edges.

You can see in the photos that I decided that the body needed to be more plump, so I added more fiber. By leaving your body and tail firm but not hard you can make these adjustments before final felting.

Remember to measure against your head, check you are happy with the shape and adjust if necessary.

ADDING A WHITE TUMMY

Before you are finished with the body, you need to add a tummy in your complementary color and then firm up the entire piece. I used roving for this bit, so I took some fiber and mixed it before creating the shape I wanted.

On the foam mat, needle the fiber into a loose egg shape and then flatten it. Flip it over and felt between your fingers to create a clean edge.

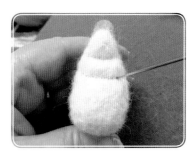

This piece needs to be thick enough so that you can't see through it, but not so thick that it bulks out the body. Remember to measure the tummy piece against the body. It should be slightly larger at this stage.

When attaching the tummy be extra careful not to over felt it. You want it attached, but you still need to sculpt the ridges. If you felt it firmly all over before adding the lines to create the ridges, it will be too hard to shape and you will end up with a line of holes!

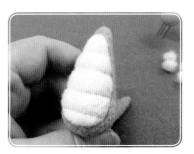

Attach the white tummy using the finer needle, and just lightly poke it all over to keep it in place. Then begin needling the lines across the top of the tummy, working back and forth to make them deeper. Don't hold the white fiber stretched tightly over the body while doing this as you won't get the nice puffy curves we are aiming for. You can then run your thumbnail along the lines firmly to help them indent more. Then felt over the lines again. Only felt the lines, not the puffy curves that you are hoping to create.

Once you have gotten all the lines in place, then you can felt the tummy all over. But if you feel that you are losing the puffiness of your curves, just tidy up the edges and leave it at that. It is better to have a nice plump tummy that's a bit soft, than a hard flat one!

MAKING THE LIMBS

The dragon's limbs are created in much the same way as the limbs for the Tabby Cat (pages 46–52). There is just one point of difference: the feet have sculpted toes. These are super simple.

ARMS

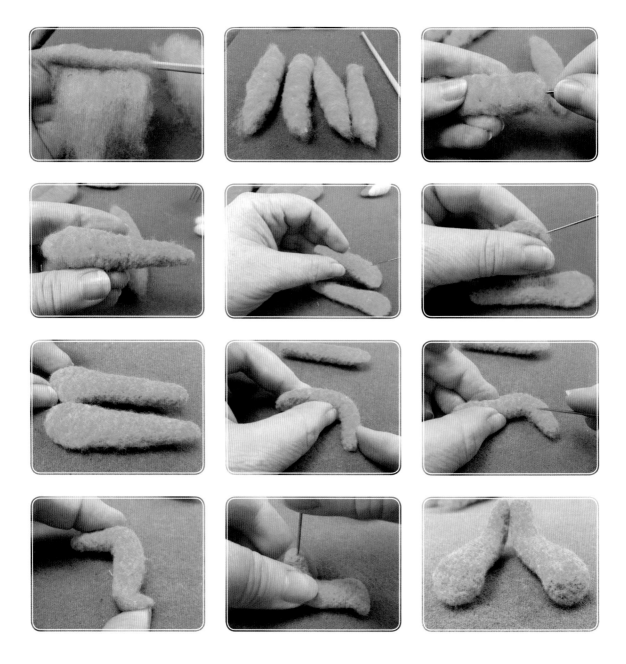

Other than that, the legs (shown in the photos below) are the same. I found it easiest to pull fiber for all four limbs at the start and roll them into shape, keeping the two larger ones for legs. Follow through the photos and refer to the Tabby Cat project should you need further instructions.

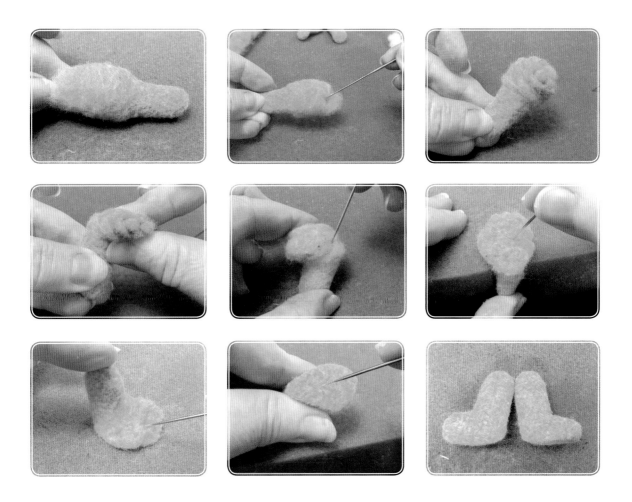

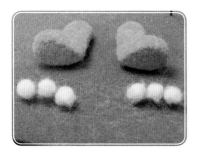  

 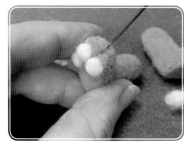 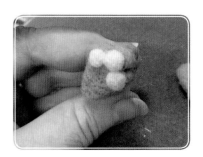

FOOT DETAILS

Roll six little balls for your toe pads, just as we did for Tabby Cat on page 49. Follow the instructions there for attaching. For the sculpted toes, you can see that they are achieved by simply felting deeply with your larger needle before the foot is too firm. I've done this after attaching the balls for the toes so that the lines are easier to place. As you can see in the photo, they go between the balls.

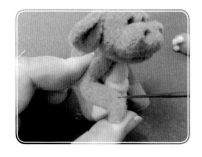

ATTACHING THE LIMBS

Attach as for the other projects (see page 50), and do the final shaping of the arms once attached (see Tabby Cat, page 52).

ADDING SPIKES ON THE BACK

The final felting step is to create the spikes down the dragon's back, just as you did for the head. You can vary them in size or keep them all small, it's up to you. The larger the spike, the more I needle it before attaching. If you wanted to make them more dinosaur-like, you could felt triangular shapes on your foam and between your fingers before attaching them to the body.

SHADING YOUR DRAGON

The final stage is to take a watercolor pencil and firmly "draw" on your finished piece to create shading. You can see the effect in the photo below right.

A soft lead pencil will leave color more easily than a regular coloring pencil. You can still use one, but they tend to rough up the surface as you have to rub the color on more firmly. If the surface does become fluffy, just lightly needle with your fine needle after coloring.

If you feel that you have made a mistake, you can sometimes trim the color off, but this is very difficult in indented areas so just add coloring lightly at first if you are unsure whether an area needs it.

He looks amazing — well done! I hope you enjoyed making your little dragon!

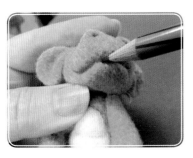

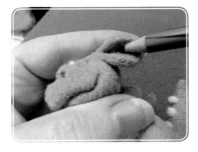

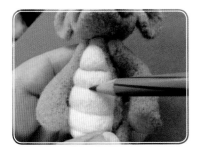

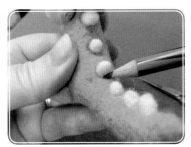

MICRO BEE BEAR

For this project we are going small! It might seem like this would be easier and quicker but that isn't usually the case with jointed needle felts. Each tiny limb has to be held between your fingertips; everything is so much smaller and fiddlier. Also, if you can master these little guys you will be able to make a larger bear in a snap! In my first book, I covered two styles of bear, so if you love this one I recommend you check them out too. In this project, you will also learn a neat trick for making tiny wings!

YOU WILL NEED:

- Fiber in two colors (I used batts for this project but actually don't recommend it for projects this size after trying it. They don't get as firm with batts and jointing is not as strong because of this, so use roving)
- Felting needles, in large and small sizes
- Foam mat
- Eye beads
- Black crochet thread for eyes and embroidering nose and antennae
- Long sewing needle and dental floss for jointing
- For wings: shrink film; permanent pen; colored pencils, chalks, etc. (optional); scissors; hole punch; sewing needle and thread

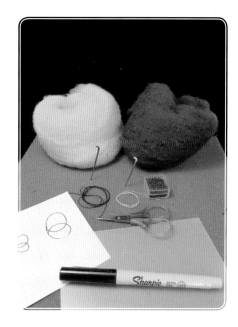

THE HEAD

Begin with a small amount of fiber for the head. How big the head is will determine how large the finished bear will be so if the first ball you make is too big, put it aside for making a bigger bear later! (My finished head is about the size of my thumbnail.)

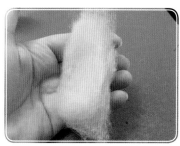

  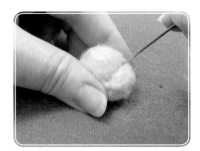

For this head, we are going to sculpt the muzzle from this first amount of fiber, rather than adding the muzzle later as a separate ball. After felting into a ball, but while it is still squishy, start to shape a muzzle by needling a line across the ball about one-third of the way up. Work back and forth over this line, and then begin felting all over with the finer needle.

You are going to be coaxing these shapes by focusing on the crease and eye area as you work around the head. If the muzzle begins to disappear as you felt into the end of it, work across the crease again to make it stand out. Keep working until you are happy with the head shape and it is fairly smooth, but not hard, as we need to add the ears.

EARS

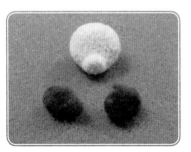

You can see what a small amount of fiber is used for the ears — the photo shows the amount for both ears not one! If working with roving, mix the amount, split into two and then start needling into soft balls with the fine needle before flattening and working on each side with light pokes to firm up. Use the finest needle you have and don't poke too deeply with these small amounts of fiber otherwise you will lose the shape. However, you will get a feel for it.

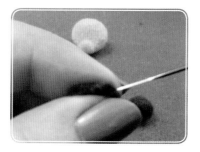

Pinch each ear between your fingers and carefully work around three-quarters of the edge, leaving a little for attaching. Are you doing OK? Poked your fingers yet?

Choose the placement for your ears and attach them as usual.

The main thing to take note of when using two colors like this is to keep them separate. So when adding the ears, you don't want lots of fluffy fiber spread over the head. You want to contain it as much as possible to keep the yellow nice and clean. This is why we needle it as a ball a little first so that the "loose" fiber isn't too fluffy.

And you can work along the edge this time to sharpen up that line and make the ear distinctive.

EYES

Next make the indentations for the eyes and attach the eye beads. Check back with the instructions for the Tabby Cat on page 43 if you need a reminder on how to attach eye beads.

 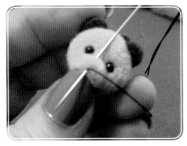 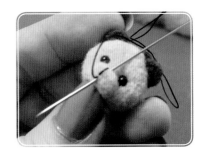

MAKING THE NOSE AND MOUTH

If you have enough thread left after adding the second eye bead, you can bring it back through and out at the nose. If you need to start with a new, longer thread, anchor it off a couple of times and then come out at the nose.

In the photograph above you can see that the needle is coming out at the bottom of where the nose will sit. Then take a stitch from the top of the nose and out at the bottom next to where the previous stitch starts.

In this way you are basically running a row of loops along to form the nose. You can work your way across and back to fill in all the gaps so don't worry if it's not perfect the first time you work across.

Once you have your nose shape, take the needle in at the top and make sure it comes out at the bottom-middle of the nose so that you can now make that downward thread you can see in the photos below.

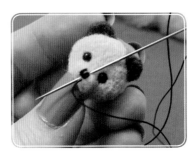 

 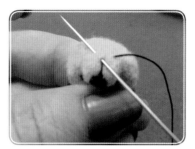 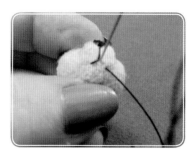

I like to hold the thread down in the direction I will be sewing it, and then take the needle in at the end of the line where the mouth will be created. You are making an upside down "Y" shape, so you will go in at the bottom of that line and out to the side. After pulling the thread through, go back up into the bottom of the long line, then out on the other side at the same height as the matching one you already made. I find it easier to turn the head upside down while doing this.

Then take the thread back through the head (don't pull too hard or the mouth will be smaller on one side). Anchor it by passing the needle back and forth across the back of the head.

MAKING THE BODY

I'm sure you're a pro at making a body by now, but if you do happen to be starting with this project, check back to one of the other projects (e.g., Tabby Cat, page 39) to see how to shape this little egg.

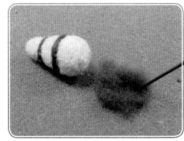
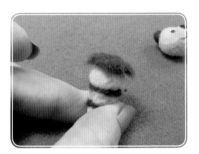

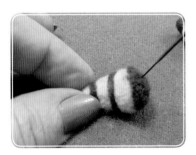

ADDING STRIPES

To do this, take a tiny amount of fiber and lay it gently around the body where you want the stripe to be. You can wrap it around loosely more than once, as long as it doesn't get too thick and bulky. You don't want to see any yellow through it. Needle lightly into place with the fine needle.

Do this for as many stripes as you want or can fit. I thought it was cute to pop some color on his bottom too. This is done in the same way as the stripes, but rubbed in your fingers to make a little pad big enough to cover the bottom of the body. Needle it a little bit to thicken it up then felt it straight on, starting in the center and working your way out.

MAKING THE LIMBS

Pull off the fiber for all four limbs so that you can be sure of the sizes. Arms should be less fiber than legs, and both should be even with the corresponding limb.

You can see in the photograph (opposite top) that I am pulling a bit of grass from my fiber with a pair of tweezers. You will often find VM (vegetable matter) in natural fibers. Tweezers are the best

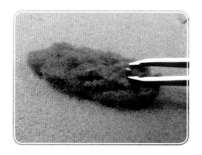  

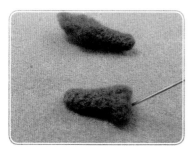  

 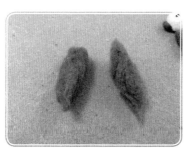 

way to take it out. Your needle will break if you use it to dig the VM out, especially if you have already started felting. In some projects it doesn't matter much, but with these tiny limbs this would no doubt be quite visible on the finished piece.

I've created the legs first, just working from the top down to the foot as was done for the Tabby Cat (page 47) and Denny Dragon (page 89). Keep your pokes shallow and light, and just use the finer needle. Remember to work on both limbs back and forth to keep them looking the same.

The arms are very simple, but you can see how tricky these little limbs are to hold and felt without drawing blood!

Joint together following the instructions as for the Tabby Cat on page 50.

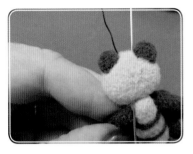

ADDING ANTENNAE

You can use a number of methods to attach the antennae. I often use wire. You can do this by cutting two short lengths and just gluing them into two small holes that you would make by needling in one place.

For these ones, we are going to use fine crochet thread to make cute, floppy antennae. This is the only time you are allowed to make knots! (Just kidding, but truly this is the only time I have ever used a knot in over 15 years of needle felting!)

Thread about 8 inches (20 cm) of thread onto your needle and make a knot at the end. Cut off the thread that is left after the knot.

Take the needle into the head right at the neck joint as far back as you can manage, this will be where the knot sits so you want to hide it as much as possible. Angle the needle so as to come out where you would like your first antenna to be and pull through firmly to hide that knot. Cut the thread, leaving as much as you want for the antenna and repeat on the other side! You could even thread tiny seed beads onto these, it's just rather fiddly getting the knots done!

MAKING TINY WINGS

For this project, I thought I would introduce you to shrink film. I use this film for making tags for my bears, but it has many uses. Shrink film comes in clear and matte white, which is what I'm using here. If you can't get hold of this, you can use the plastic packaging you buy some of your foods in. Have a practice with food-grade

containers such as the ones your tomatoes might come in. This plastic is crushable, so if you were to stand on it, it would crumple. Thicker plastics would snap and shatter, so those aren't suitable.

To make the wings, use a rough template. The plastic will shrink to about half its original size, so I drew what I wanted and then blew it up larger — to about double. These are tiny amounts of plastic, so you could always make a few sizes and then use the ones you like, saving the other pairs for future projects.

I drew the wings out with a fine permanent marker, then flipped the film over and traced it the other way around so I would have a matching pair. Because this plastic becomes very white and opaque, you need to draw the lines on both sides or only one will have the outline showing once sewn on. You could also add some pattern or color on these before shrinking. Experiment with iridescent chalks and pastels, or colored pencils.

Don't forget to add a punched hole for sewing the wings on!

The wings go into the oven for just a few moments, and you can watch them as they shrink down. (See the manufacturer's instructions for temperatures.) To attach them, I have just anchored off my thread across the body a few times, then sewn them on like a button. Super easy!

I hope you have enjoyed this project. You can adapt it to make all sorts of tiny bears and friends. If you add a safety pin or jewelry clasp at the back, they make cute brooches or friends to carry around.

LADY LINARA DOLL

For this project, you will learn to use pipe cleaners as a new way to wrap and attach parts to your sculpture, and also how to create hair. This is my take on the Waldorf doll, which traditionally has no face and is made with natural materials. This doll is robust enough for children's play and it's very versatile. You can make many styles once you learn the basic techniques, and perhaps create a whole family!

YOU WILL NEED:

- ◆ Core fiber
- ◆ Skin color fiber, preferably in a rope (roving) rather than batts
- ◆ Roving or merino for hair
- ◆ Colored fiber for her outfit
- ◆ Needles in large and fine grades
- ◆ Foam mat
- ◆ Pipe cleaner

THE HEAD

Begin by mixing the core fiber for the head. You are aiming to needle a ball approximately the size of a table tennis ball 1½ inches (4 cm) across. The head should be reasonably firm but not hard when done. If you need to, you can add layers of core fiber to make the head bigger.

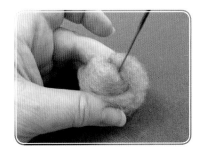

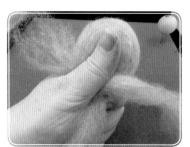

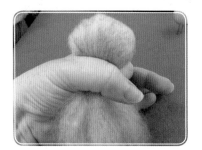

To add the skin color, pull off at least three lengths of fiber and lay them on your foam mat as shown. Slip your hand under the middle of this "star" shape and pick it up with the felted ball in the middle. Then close your hand with the wool now wrapped around the ball.

Holding the loose fiber, take a sliver of roving and wrap it between the ball and your hand, while firmly holding the fiber on the ball. You can add more fiber to wind around if it's not firm enough or not creating enough of a "neck" shape. It should hold on its own, but you can needle a few times to keep it in place if you wish.

Holding all the loose fiber in your hand, start needling the head with the larger felting needle if you can. The finer one will be all right to use if your large needle isn't slipping in easily enough.

Remember when working with a ball to steady it as you work. It can break your needle very quickly if it suddenly rolls mid poke!

Work the entire surface until you are happy that it is smooth and not dimpled with holes.

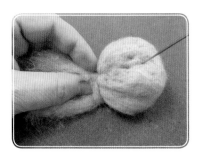

MAKING THE ARMS AND TORSO

Take the pipe cleaner and fold the ends in toward the middle. How far you fold will affect how long the arms will be (and the arm length will depend on how large your doll is going to be). At this stage, assess the arm length by placing the folded pipe cleaner below the head and see if the length looks correct.

If you are making a smaller doll, you might want to cut the pipe cleaner in half with wire cutters and then just roll the ends in to create hands after you have wrapped them with fiber. As this is a reasonably large doll, it will use the entire pipe cleaner.

Once you have confirmed the right length for your doll, fold the pipe cleaner lightly as the next step is to open it up again and wrap it with slivers of skin-colored fiber. You don't need to cover the entire wire, just the area where the hands will be (as this is the only part of the arm that shows). So perhaps an inch (2.5 cm) either side of each bend.

Hold the end of the fiber against the wire with one hand, then wrap firmly with the other, working toward the bend and then past it. If you can see the "fuzz" of the pipe cleaner, do another layer so the arm is well covered.

You can now bend the pipe cleaner firmly to create your hand. Then take more fiber and start wrapping from the unfolded end. Wrap in the direction of the bend so that it all holds together securely and there is only a little of the bend showing.

Do this for both sides.

ATTACHING THE ARMS

Take the head, split the loose fiber in two, then push the covered pipe cleaner up into the split you just made. This will create a torso with an arm on each side.

Adjust the pipe cleaner so that the arms are the same length, then wrap the torso as shown with core or skin fiber. Using your large felting needle, felt all over to hold the arms in place.

Working over pipe cleaners is quite straightforward and doesn't pose as much of a problem as you might expect. You just need to be careful that if your needle slips in between twists of wire, that you pull it out carefully. And remember to work straight in and out. You should still have some loose fiber below the pipe cleaner. This is needed for attaching the lower half of the body, so leave it unfelted.

Remember that you can build the torso up, adding and needling as you go until you are happy with the shape and size.

We will also be adding another layer over the top of the torso to create the clothing, so it will be firmer and thicker after that as well.

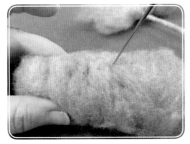

MAKING AND ATTACHING THE BODY

Taking core fiber again, create the body or "skirt" of the doll. Even though I'm not using batts for this part of the project, I have wrapped the fiber around my skewer to create a firm cylinder as this is a quicker method.

Needle the cylinder to create a thinner end and a thicker end (this will be the end the doll stands on). The body needs to be fairly firm and flat on the bottom so that your figure will stand well. It needs to be wider at the bottom for balance as well. Needle until firm, but not hard.

Attach the body in the same way as the arms were attached. Split the loose fiber from below the arms and cover the top of the cone-shaped body. Spread the fiber out so that it covers the top evenly and then needle it in place.

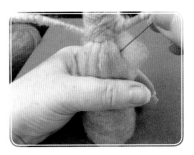

If you don't have much fiber left for this step, you may have to add pieces that cover both the torso and the top of the body to create the attachment.

Once you are happy with how everything is attached and the firmness of the piece, you can add the final layers.

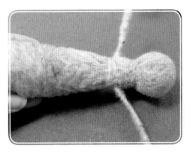

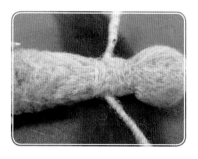

ADDING THE CLOTHING

First, add the wool around the torso to create the top of the dress. You can wrap the fiber any way you like, but if you come straight across the back and then down each side at the front it creates a V-neck, which looks more like clothing.

If you are using batts for this top layer (as I did), just wrap it around the torso and start needling. You can use fiber that is in rope or "sliver" form, just remember to mix it well first and create a large loose bed of fiber that you can wrap your piece in.

Needle all over, changing down to the finer needle as the surface begins to smooth. Don't make it completely hard, as you will want to add some finer decorations to finish off your doll.

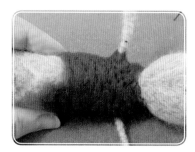

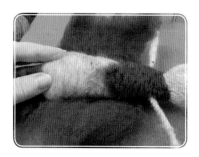
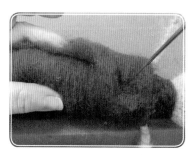

Wrap the arms as well, leaving the hands free. Poke your needle from the arm into the body and vice versa so that the sleeve attaches to the body of the dress.

Poking straight down from the hand, as shown, will create a nice little cuff or edge to your sleeve.

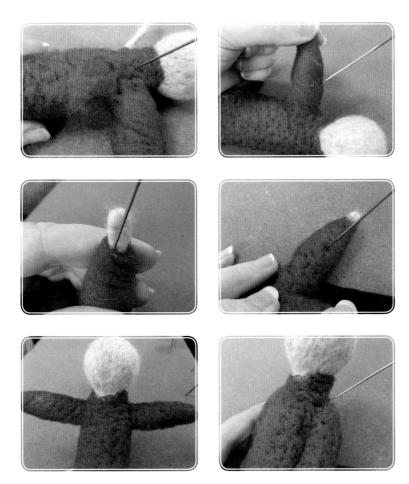

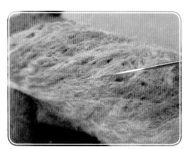

DECORATING

The fiber I wanted to use for decorating the doll was a gorgeous merino blend. As I wanted to keep the ribbons of color in the layer, I didn't mix it. Instead, I pulled off a length that would wrap from the front, over one shoulder and down the back. I then made a little hole for the arm to fit through and slipped it on.

Needling this on takes more time, as you need to use only the finer needle and scatter a lot of shallow pokes all over until it is well attached.

Fiber that lies only in one direction, as it does here, tends to just sit on the surface and so pulls off easily. This is why I don't often work this way, but in this case it makes such a nice decorative element I couldn't resist! This is not such a good idea if the doll is going to be played with, as it would wear off quite quickly.

You can also decorate the dress with embroidery, needle felt some flowers on with just small balls of fiber, do some bead work — in fact, anything you like!

HAIR

The final touch is to create some hair for your "lady." I don't believe long flowing hair like this can be achieved with batts so I used roving. You could do a short hairstyle or use yarn which you can actually needle on in a similar way to what I do in these instructions.

Pull a length of fiber long enough to cover the head and reach down each side of the doll. Hold loosely in place and needle a parting down the center of the head with the large needle. A side part is equally attractive. Just make sure the part lines are straight and go back over them a couple of times to catch in all the fiber. Take the parting right down to the back of the neck.

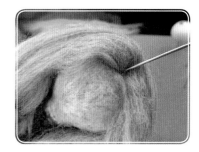

For this doll, I have done little buns on the side. Twisting the fiber away from the face, hold it at roughly below ear level and keep twisting until it begins to twist up on itself, creating the little buns almost on its own. You need to keep hold of the fiber the entire time or it will unravel.

Wind the ends around the bun and then needle into place. Try not to needle the twist directly or it will spoil the effect, but do needle around, underneath and through the middle of the twists. You could also do plaits and leave them loose with a ribbon at the end, or twist them up and needle them into place.

In my first book, *Needle Felting From Basics to Bears*, there are other ideas for creating hairstyles and clothing for felted figures, so do check it out if you haven't already!

POTS OF JOY

These cute little gardens can be made in so many ways. The size shown here uses terra-cotta pots about 2¾ inches (7 cm) tall, but I have also done ones just over an inch (3 cm) tall. You don't have to use pots either, you could use teacups or anything with an indentation (I've seen micro ones done in walnut shells!). You could also felt the entire thing and not use a container at all. It is totally up to you. Here are two ideas for decorating, and I hope you will be inspired to design amazing gardens and landscapes of your own!

YOU WILL NEED:

- Core or cheap fiber to fill the pots
- Wools in assorted colors
- Felting needles
- Foam mat
- Containers (in this case I used terra-cotta pots)

LET'S BEGIN!

Start by stuffing as much core fiber as you can firmly into the container. It should appear that you have far too much and that it will never fit, but, of course, we know that once you start felting it shrinks down. Start felting with your larger needle until it reaches the height you want.

Mix the fiber for your grass and pop it straight onto the core. It also needs to look like way too much so that it doesn't shrink away when you felt it and show the core. Add more as necessary for any patches that need it.

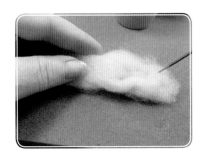

MAKING THE MUSHROOM

I've made this mushroom by using a light beige fiber and felting it into a soft stump. You need a very loose end to add the top onto, and the other end still needs to be soft so that you can felt it into the "ground."

Make the top by felting a fat disk from your red fiber. If it flattens too much as you felt, you can add another ball of fiber to plump it up (as I did in these photos). Just pop the extra fiber straight on and keep needling, changing down to your fine needle when ready to work it until nice and smooth.

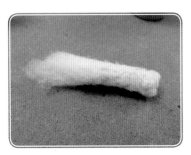

Fluff out the fiber on the stump ready to attach to the top. Don't poke too deeply when attaching or the lighter colored fiber of the stump will come out through the red and make strange little hairs on the top. As you can see, I wanted more beige under the top so I added another layer and felted it gently until smooth.

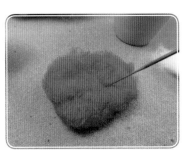

Pinch off tiny bits of white fiber to make the spots on top and felt them in with your finer needle.

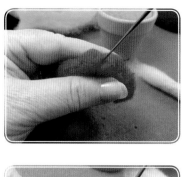

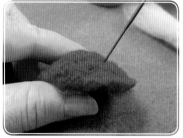

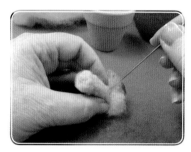

ATTACHING TO THE BASE

Hopefully you can see that the middle of the stump is firmer than the ends. You will want to attach the mushroom without flyaway hairs spreading across the green "grass," so felt directly and deeply down through the stump and into the base with the larger needle.

Work your way around the base, changing down to the finer needle once you are sure that it is well attached. Work until smooth.

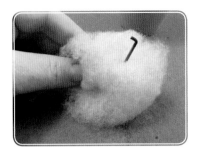

MAKING THE HOUSE

I wasn't overly happy with the house and if I were to make it again, I would probably make it a bit fatter. So feel free to make a squarer shape for your house (mine is more rectangular).

I used the same color as the mushroom stalk for the house, but you could do it in any color.

Felt a rough ball shape and then begin making flat sides by turning it evenly and felting in one place to create a flat area.

As with the mushroom stalk, you want both ends of the house to be less felted than the middle.

Mix and felt the fiber for the roof. I decided to do a cone shape, but you could do any shape or height you want.

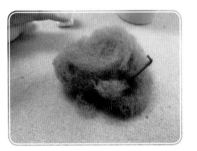

 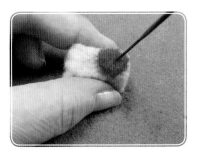 

I've then taken a little red fiber and used it to make a door. You could add windows, or other embellishments to your house. The larger the house, the more detail you can add.

Then put the roof on by felting deeply down into the house. Then work all over with the finer needle.

Oops, you know what? This house looks too tall. Before the roof was well attached, I decided to make a change. I pulled it off and then cut the house shorter before putting the roof back on. Because the roof was still quite loosely felted this worked well. If it was felted more firmly, the two might not have attached together.

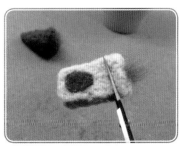

TIP

As I was felting I realized that my foam was rather messy and the red fiber was going to get mixed up in the beige. So I pulled the red out. You might find that you need to do this during projects with very different colors, or between projects. It also helps the foam to last longer.

The house is then attached to the base the same way that you added the mushroom.

Some little bushes can be added, made from balls of green fiber. Lightly felt them and needle in place.

I also added a little path going up to the house.

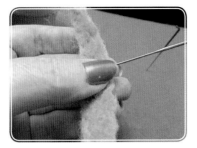

BLADES OF GRASS

When I had finished my house and mushroom, I decided that the pot needed something extra! So, taking the same fiber as for the ground, I flat felted two long pieces of batts into the shapes I wanted. You can do this with roving, just make sure that you mix it well. You might need to felt it for longer to get rid of all the long fibers that will be visible.

In either case, you can trim the work with scissors once it is firmly felted. Keep one end loose and then felt it on. I quite liked my leaves floppy, but if you wanted them to stand straighter you could glue pipe cleaners up the back of the blades. Then they would also be bendable to the shape you want!

This is a great project for trying things out and for using your imagination.

ANOTHER IDEA TO TRY

As well as the above supplies you will also need:

* Pipe cleaners
* Wire cutters
* Multi-purpose glue
* Black marker, or similar
* Orange marker, or similar

To begin, fill the container as for the previous project, including adding the green fiber for the grass.

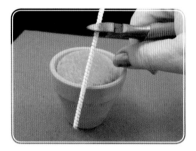

MAKING A TREE

Cut a length of pipe cleaner an inch (2.5 cm) longer than you would like your tree to be to allow for attaching. Then wrap the pipe cleaner with a fine strand of fiber. I've gone up the length and back to ensure it is well covered. You don't need to felt this much if you wind fairly tightly, just enough to hold the ends in place.

Now pull and mix some fiber to create a small ball. Remember that you can always make it a little bigger as you go.

Hold it against the trunk to see if you are happy with the size.

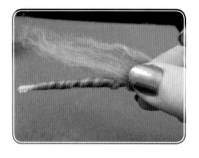

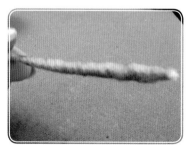

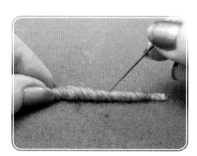

Needle until squishy but firm, then create an indentation by felting in one place with the larger needle.

Poke the trunk into this indentation and, while holding it on your foam mat, needle down, taking the fiber from the trunk into the ball. Then work around the ball to help secure this join.

I decided another little ball in the middle would be cute, so taking another fine length of fiber I wrapped it loosely around the trunk, keeping it in the same place so that it creates some height and doesn't spread along the trunk.

You can help keep the ball defined by felting along the edges where it attaches to the trunk.

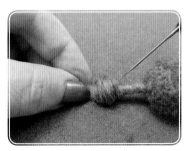

I used my felting needle to help decide on the placement and angle of the tree, then needled in one place to create an indent. Try poking the trunk into the hole. Is it deep enough? If you have trouble getting it deep enough, you can snip into the hole with small scissors and try again. To attach, I put glue on the trunk and pushed it into the hole.

MAKING THE POND

Mix the fiber for your water, then felt into shape on your foam mat.

Attach with your finer needle, working all around the shape and defining the edges.

As you can see, I also made a second tree and then added some balls to create bushes around my pond.

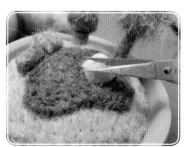

ADDING A DUCK

Take a little yellow fiber and felt a small oblong shape. Then attach it to the water, forming a bend along what will be its back.

This little duck took a lot of patience and experimentation. Just keep working over the shape with your fine needle using light pokes. I made a tiny ball for the head and attached that while pinching what would be the beak in my fingers and felting that shape lightly.

Use scissors to help refine the shape.

Then use a black marker to create the eyes. Just push lightly into the fiber and turn to make a dot.

For the beak, brush the orange marker on the fiber until the color is built up to your liking.

Use your imagination, practice and remember there will always be someone who loves and appreciates what you make, even if sometimes it's not you!

ABOUT THE AUTHOR

THE BASICS

My name is Liza, and I'm the middle-aged mother of three who became addicted to needle felting almost 15 years ago. I live in Hamilton, New Zealand, and have done so for most of my life. My husband is a computer addict, which is lucky as that is also his job. I put up with his computer quirks and he puts up with my addiction to small furry animals, of which we have quite a few, including dogs, guinea pigs and rabbits. Our most exotic pets are a pair of chinchillas.

Our lounge is where I like to work on my creations. It's not always the most productive space, but I just couldn't work shut away in another room. I need to be with the rest of the family, even if it means a few pokes in the fingers while I try to watch a movie! I do most of my work at night, as I am rather a night owl and love to keep my hands busy.

HOW I STARTED FELTING

In 2004 I was a certified Parchment Craft Teacher, and was teaching night classes at a local college. It was during one of these classes that a student showed me what she had been making at home.

Her bears were lovely, and she assured me they were fun and easy to make. This piqued my interest as I loved bears, but wasn't having that much luck with the sewn kind.

The next time I was at a craft show, I looked out for the lady who was selling kits and books, and after making my first creation from a kit, I bought her book. I was then firmly on track to a woolly addiction, and spent many years refining my style, experimenting with lots of different ideas and techniques, and basically trying to find my niche in this art of sculpting with wool.

HOW I FIND INSPIRATION

When I first started out, I used to do lots of online searches, looking for bears of all descriptions, trying out different paw shapes, muzzle sizes and ear positions. I would keep a reference copy of anything that I liked the look of. I accumulated hundreds

of pages of ideas and inspiration. I tried to never replicate anyone else's work, but rather just picked a part of the bear that I liked and mixed it with other styles to see how it would turn out. (Most of these first bears were given away, but I do still have the very first bear I ever made.)

I feel it's very important to find your own style as an artist; some may say that imitation is the sincerest form of flattery, but I say it's just copying, and people need to do their own work, find their own niche, and create their own style. The wonderful thing with needle-felted bears as opposed to sewn ones is that there are no patterns, no one else is using the same pattern as you and turning out the same bear over and over again in different colors, or with different accessories as the only things that make them one of a kind. Needle-felted works are truly unique, whether you are making bears, dogs, cats, or monsters! Embrace this and go wild! People will love your passion, as it always shows in the finished work.

For myself, my fiber inspires me. If I'm feeling a bit stuck and can't think of anything I want to make, I go to my stash! I have four 16-gallon (60-liter) plastic boxes stacked around the house. My stash is the result of 10 years of hoarding, searching, craft shows, trading, and hours and hours of online surfing. I love unique fibers, and I adore gorgeous blends that no one else makes. So while I have all the commercial dyed fibers available here in New Zealand, I also have fabulous back-yard dyed Romneys, Australian blended silks and merinos, US merino tops, along with alpaca, angora, and more.

Pulling out colors, trying them together, making unusual combos; all these things inspire me to make something new. I need to keep my work original for myself and for my customers. Recently, I made a super cute little yellow duck, which I put up on my Facebook page and sold within an hour. After that, I got four orders for little yellow ducks. I think I made another two, and just couldn't do it anymore. I guess that's why I find it so surprising that I have been doing this for so long — I have made around 1,000 bears and still haven't gotten bored! It's a truly exciting craft, even after all this time.

MY FAVORITE CREATIONS

I've had a few bears over the years that have been hard to part with. Some I have made for orders, and hated to send them away. Some I made for myself, only to have a customer fall in love and I just couldn't say no. I've learned to keep some as "not for sale" for a little while, so that I can enjoy them before they have to go. That seems to be working for me, as now I can make a bear that I love, and think I will never sell, but after a few months I'm ready for him to find a new home.

I guess Zachary would be one of my first favorites. He was the Little Handfuls mascot for my first 10 years, and has only recently been retired. The new mascot, or face, of Little Handfuls keeps changing but always incorporates some of my favorite features, like big feet, large bellies, and soulful faces. People often ask how I can give away such lovely little creations, and the honest answer is, sometimes I can't! But knowing that they are going to awesome new homes really helps; all my customers are wonderful.

WHERE TO FROM HERE

Well, over the years I have had a number of accomplishments or milestones. I've taught night classes and started my Facebook business. I have traveled to teach lovely ladies and their friends, and attended more shows than I can count. I've been on television for a craft segment which has been aired a number of times. I've won awards for my work, written for magazines in New Zealand and overseas, and been featured on multiple websites. I've spoken to large groups and taught in a private girls' school. I've sold my work in boutique gift stores, sent bears all around the world and received wonderful emails from people who love what I do.

Fifteen years ago I wouldn't have thought any of these things were likely to happen, so I suppose that the next 15 years could be filled with as many exciting things as the last. I have the success of another book to think about, and I would really love to travel overseas and do some international bear shows as there are so many great ones out there. And this year I will be starting a Patreon group where people will have access to lessons from me via their own computers, and much more.

Writing these two books has been a lot of work as well as a lot of fun. So as long as people like the projects and continue to find them interesting and useful, I am happy to impart more of my sculpting wisdom to the world!

I hope you enjoy working through my book and thanks for your support.

Liza Adams, 2020